THE YEAR 2000

THE YEAR 2000
All Your Fears and Questions Answered

Linda Moore

Ottenheimer
PUBLISHERS

Created and manufactured by Ottenheimer Publishers, Inc.

5 Park Center Court
Owings Mills, Maryland 21117

Printed in the United States.
ML100M L K J I H G F E D C B A
ISBN 0-8241-0286-X

Table of Contents

Introduction

What Is This Event We Call the Millennium?

What is a millennium? By the dictionary definition, all that the word *millennium* means is the passing of a thousand years. Yet, as the year 2000 approaches, many people are filled with fear and believe that something terrible is about to happen. Will the world end in a fiery nuclear explosion? Will floods and earthquakes rock the earth? Will the Day of Judgment be at hand? Other people look at the approaching millennium in the opposite way, as a time when great events will take place and a Golden Age of peace and prosperity will arrive. For many others, the first day of the year 2000 will be greeted with a shrug of the shoulders and a casual "So what?" January 1, 2000, some people say, will be just another New Year's Day, even if it is a good excuse to celebrate. There are even some people who insist that the millennium begins not on the first day of the year 2000 but in the year 2001. We will examine why they think so in chapter 1.

But when the clock strikes midnight on December 31, 1999, even people who aren't expecting anything special to happen will find it hard not to take notice. For many mysterious reasons, human beings have always marked the end of a period in time—whether a year, a decade, or a century—with great fanfare. We celebrate. We look back on where we've been and think forward to where we're going. And we make predictions, both positive and negative. Imagine, then, how much fanfare will greet the passing of *a thousand years*. Not many people in the whole history of the world have had the chance to witness an event like that. And we are among the chosen few.

We may get a sense of how special we are when we realize just how long people have been thinking about the arrival of the millennium. More than a century ago, in 1892, a commentator for *The Spectator*, a London newspaper, was already wondering what that great moment would be like. "Even now," he wrote, "the idea of that *annus mirabilus* [miraculous year], the Year of Grace 2000, begins to affect us. We feel that if we could live to witness its advent, we should witness an immense event. We should almost expect something to happen in the cosmos, so that we might read the great date written in the skies." The writer sounds as if he was almost envious that he wouldn't be alive to see the year 2000. And it's interesting that he felt that some heavenly sign would mark the moment. It seems that prophecies of some supernatural happening for the millennium are nothing new!

But why should we feel that the heavens should take notice? After all, the millennium is a man-made event—only people tell time. As the German author Thomas Mann once wrote, "Time has no divisions to mark its passage. There is never a thunderstorm or blare of trumpets to announce the beginning of a new month or year. Even when a new century begins, it is only we mortals who ring bells and fire off pistols." Why do we make such a big deal about a date that, as we will see in chapter 1, was based on a mistaken calculation about the birth of Jesus that could have resulted in a different date altogether? And if the millennium marks two thousand years since the birth of Jesus, why will people all over the world—Christians and non-Christians alike—celebrate its passing? Most important, why do so many people feel that something either great or terrible will happen when the millennium arrives? Where did this idea come from? Are our fears and hopes justified? And how should we prepare for the Big Event?

In this book, we will explore answers to all of these questions and more. We will look at the many ways in which the arrival of the year 2000 will affect our lives. We will review the many prophecies and predictions that are now being made about the millennium—from the wild and wacky to the truly troubling—and see which ones may come true. We will look, too, at the various Christian beliefs about the millennium, as well as at what the event has meant to other religions around the world, past and present. We will find out how people greeted the last millennium in the year 1000. Were those long-ago people afraid that the end of the world was coming, or was it just another day to them? And we will see how and why the passing of a thousand years came to be such a powerful, important event in the first place—an event that so many people the world over are already preparing for with fear and wonder, terror and promise.

Did you ever calculate just how old you will be when the year 2000 arrives? Did you ever stop and think, "Where will I be and what will I have accomplished by that great day in the future?" If you have, then you, too, have felt that somehow this event is special. And this book is for you.

Chapter 1

What Is So Special About the Year 2000?

As we saw in the Introduction, people have been thinking about and looking forward to the year 2000 for a very long time. Today, we are bombarded with reminders that the millennium is coming. It seems that each new day brings a special edition of a magazine or TV show about the event. Politicians, scientists, and journalists constantly talk about what will happen in the twenty-first century. A flood of merchandise—from coffee mugs to T-shirts to calendars—has arrived to commemorate the arrival of this special year. With all the excitement, it's difficult *not* to think about the year 2000 as a great moment in human history. But why? Isn't it just another day on the calendar?

Well, yes and no. It's true that the year 2000 is a man-made event and that another day could just as easily have ended up being the first day of January 2000. As we will see, the date was calculated by someone who was measuring time based on the birth of Jesus, but he got the date wrong. Certainly, nothing in nature recognizes that any particular year is special. Nature is unchanging—the sun rises and sets every day, and the four seasons repeat their cycle—and January 1, 2000, probably will be a cold winter day in much of North America, just like every other New Year's Day. But the human need to mark a particular day or year as special is as old as humankind. And by that measure, the year 2000 will be very special indeed.

The year 2000 is a powerful symbol of the future, a date to mark the beginning of a new era in human history. For Christians, it will mark the biggest birthday celebration ever for Jesus Christ. And it will be the biggest New Year's celebration since people began recognizing centuries as distinct historical periods—about 700 years ago. Perhaps most important, it will be the first time that the whole world will celebrate a millennium together. A thousand years ago, all people did not count time in the same way, if they even had calendars at all. Now, because nearly everyone everywhere recognizes the same calendar (the Gregorian, which we will discuss a little later in this chapter) as a standard measure of time, everyone everywhere will be united in their recognition of the year 2000 as the beginning of the third one-thousand-year period in the history of the human race.

What is a millennium, anyway?

The word *millennium* comes from the Latin word for "thousand," *mille*, and can refer to any thousand-year span of time. Thus, the millennium we will celebrate marks the beginning of the third thousand-year period since the birth of Jesus Christ. But this simple definition does not entirely explain why today we attach so much importance to the thousand-year mark as a measurement of time. Why don't we make a big deal, for example, of the 1,998th birthday of Jesus? And our simple definition of the word doesn't quite explain why the millennium is so often associated with visions of the end of time or of a Golden Age. We will look at these mysteries next.

Why do we assign special importance to decades, centuries, and millennia?

One reason the millennium receives so much attention is because of our numerical system, which is based on ten, the decimal system. The special position occupied by ten stems from the number of human fingers. Thus, it is perfectly natural for us to categorize large units of time around that number. For example, we mark milestones in our lives by decades (turning forty is much more likely to cause a midlife crisis than turning thirty-nine or forty-one, even though logically we don't feel much different). We categorize historical periods by the same method. If the arrival of a new decade (*deca* means "ten" in Greek) makes us feel as if we are entering a new period in time when everything will change (we all know how different the innocent 1950s were from the free-spirited 1960s), the arrival of ten times ten decades (a new century) makes us feel ten times more so! And the arrival of a millennium—well, the kinds of changes a hundred times ten will bring are almost beyond the imagination.

Why is the millennium associated with the end of time?

Another important reason why the millennium feels different, and why it is so closely associated with heightened hopes and fears, is its biblical meaning. In the final book of the Bible, Revelation, "millennium" refers to the prophesied reign of Christ after his return to the earth, bringing "a new heaven and a new earth" (Revelation 21:1) and a rule of perfect peace and justice from a New Jerusalem. According to Revelation, this reign will be followed by a terrible battle between the forces of Satan and the forces of God, during which a number of horrifying events will come to pass, destroying the wicked of the earth. Then the Final Judgment will come. We will discuss Revelation in detail in chapter 5.

Is there a connection between the biblical millennium and the year 2000?

Although there is no necessary connection between the calendar's turning of a thousand years and a predicted return to paradise, many people do connect the two meanings of the word *millennium*, which explains why the approach of the year 2000 has been accompanied by predictions and prophecies of the end of time. The end of a cycle of time has always held great power over the human imagination. Ever since people began to recognize centuries as a measure of time (around the twelfth or thirteenth century), the last years of a century have been greeted with general feelings of fear and excitement. Imagine how much these feelings increase when we are talking about the end of a thousand-year cycle! John Naisbitt described this effect in his best-selling book *Megatrends 2000*:

> Already we have fallen under its dominion. The year 2000 is operating like a powerful magnet on humanity, reaching down into the 1990s and intensifying the decade. It is amplifying emotions, accelerating change, heightening awareness, and compelling us to reexamine ourselves, our values, and our institutions.

Those who connect the description of the millennium in Revelation and our coming millennium often predict dire events for the year 2000. In chapter 2, we will see what some of these current predictions are and whether they might be true. But whether the predictions are scary or hopeful, many people agree that the end of the millennium is a time for taking stock of our place in the world.

Why do some people say the millennium begins in 2001?

You have probably heard many people insist that the last day of the twentieth century will be December 31, 2000, and that the third millennium will not actually start until January 1, 2001. Technically speaking, these people are correct. Why? The answer has to do with a certain sixth-century Roman monk named Dionysius Exiguus, or, as his name is translated from Latin into English, Dennis the Short.

In 525 A.D., Pope St. John I asked Dennis to settle once and for all a long-standing dispute about the proper day for Easter. Dennis worked for months in Roman numerals, calculating a new basis for the Christian calendar. The result was the invention of an all-new calendar for computing years, and it is the same calendar we use today. Dennis is responsible for why we count years according to the birth of Christ—designating years before Christ's birth as either "B.C." (before Christ) or "B.C.E." (before the common era), and years *after* his birth as either "A.D." (*anno Domini*—in the year of the Lord) or "C.E." (of the common era).

The only problem was that Dennis named Jesus' birth as 1 *anno Domini*, or 1 A.D., instead of 0 A.D. Therefore, whenever we start a new decade, century, or millennium, it really begins with a one. But this unfortunate and awkward counting system isn't really Dennis's fault because there are no zeros in Roman numerals. Experts are not even sure that the zero was even in use back in Dennis's time.

To further add to the confusion, Dennis made another miscalculation that *was* his fault. He got the year of the birth of Jesus wrong. Using the year of the establishment of Rome as a starting point, as people did at that time, Dennis calculated that Jesus was born 753 years later. But we know that King Herod, who was definitely alive during Christ's time on earth, died 750 years after the founding of Rome. Dennis had to be wrong by at least four years. In other words, using Dennis's calendar, Jesus Christ was actually born in 4 B.C.—a very confusing thought! Thus, Dennis has caused a lot of conflict over the year 2000.

Will it be the year 2000 on all calendars?

No. In fact, technically speaking, it will be the year 2000 only on the Gregorian calendar, which counts years from the birth of Christ, according to Dennis the Short's calculation. On the Chinese calendar, the year 2000 will be the year 4698; on the Islamic calendar, it will be 1420 to 1421; and on the Jewish calendar, it will be 5760 to 5761. Why is this? Because each of these calendars counts years from a date other than the birth of Jesus. For example, the Jewish calendar counts years from the creation of the world (or *anno mundi*, Latin for "year of the world"), which in Judaism is reckoned to have occurred 3,761 years before the birth of Christ. However, today these calendars are used mostly for religious purposes—for example, to determine religious holidays. We think of the Gregorian calendar as *the* calendar because it is almost universally accepted and used for business, science, travel, communications, and governmental affairs.

How long has the Gregorian calendar been in use?

The Gregorian calendar was introduced in 1582. It is named after Pope Gregory XIII, who ordered that a new calendar replace the Julian calendar, named for its inventor, the Roman emperor Julius Caesar. Both calendars were based on the twelve-month cycle we know today, except that Pope Gregory added an extra day to the calendar every four years (what we know as leap year) to accommodate the solar year. Since the Julian was the calendar Christians used at the time of Dennis the Short, it began counting the years from 1 A.D., after Dennis's calculations. The Gregorian calendar, of course, followed suit.

Why will most people celebrate the millennium in the year 2000?

Because most people recognize and use the Gregorian calendar, Christians, Jews, Muslims, Hindus, Buddhists—people of all faiths and nationalities—will be celebrating the new millennium. And despite the fact that technically the millennium begins on January 1, 2001, most of these people will be celebrating in the year 2000. Why? It just seems to feel right. Perhaps it goes back to our attachment to the decimal system, or perhaps it is because historically people feel that figures ending in round numbers carry a sense of completion.

In his book *Questioning the Millennium*, Stephen Jay Gould comes up with a simple solution to the 2000/2001 dilemma: Why not proclaim that the first decade contained only nine years? After all, he reasons, no one living back then recognized a decade as a unit of time anyway. It's as good an answer to the problem as any.

There also are some people who feel that celebrating the birthday of Jesus Christ in the year 2000 is wrong, since Dennis the Short got Jesus' actual birth year wrong. But if we follow this logic, we should no longer celebrate Christmas on December 25 either, since that date is only an estimate of the actual day of Christ's birth.

What will we celebrate in the year 2000?

The year 2000 will mark the anniversary of a thousand years of remarkable human achievement. Even if we look back only on the twentieth century, we can see that there are many landmarks to celebrate. From the invention of the automobile to the discovery of the polio vaccine to the end of Communism in Russia, ours has been one of the most important centuries in the history of the world. When we look to the past thousand years, the list of events to celebrate becomes nearly endless. We will discuss some of those events in chapter 8, but for now we can mention just one event important for all Americans: the discovery of America in 1492.

The year 2000 is cause for celebration as we look ahead as well. We can celebrate the fact that we have survived another century and are now ready to cross into a new era. This anniversary will be a great time to look back on how far we have come and to look forward to the challenges that await us.

Finally, the year 2000 marks the anniversary of the birth of Jesus Christ. For Christians all over the world, Christ's arrival in the world roughly two thousand years ago is the most important event in human history. And because his teachings and philosophy have been such an influence on the history of the world, it is a time for everyone—Christian and non-Christian alike—to think about the effect the life of Jesus has had over the past two thousand years.

How will we celebrate the year 2000?

Hundreds of important celebrations of the year 2000 are in the planning stages right now. While many people will plan to celebrate with perhaps only a bigger-than-usual New Year's Eve party for family and friends, others will want to mark the occasion by attending large community gatherings to be held in cities and towns all over the world. And for those who want to celebrate in a very special way with a *really* big group of people, a number of events throughout the year will host at least one million people. Some of these events will continue throughout the year 2000 and into 2001:

* **Times Square 2000.** More than one million people are expected to join Dick Clark in New York City for the New Year's Eve 1999 Celebration in Times Square. Giant television screens throughout the twelve-block downtown area will broadcast a twenty-four-hour global celebration called "The Crossroads of the World." The broadcast will salute the coming of the new millennium in all twenty-four time zones by showing New Year's scenes from around the world. Times Square 2000 will begin at 7:00 A.M. eastern standard time on December 31, 1999, when the giant screens will broadcast the arrival of the New Year in the Fiji Islands. In addition to those who will be watching in Times Square, 250 million television viewers from all over the world also are expected to watch the event.

* **Holy Year 2000.** Vatican City in Rome will celebrate the Great Jubilee of the Incarnation of Christ as declared by Pope John Paul II. The special celebrations, which will run from December 24, 1999, to January 1, 2000, are expected to attract more than 30 million tourists.
* **Holy Land 2000.** A total of four million visitors are expected to visit Palestine and Israel during the year 2000 to commemorate the two thousandth anniversary of the birth of Christ. Special events are being hosted in Bethlehem, Nazareth, and Jerusalem from 1999 to 2001.
* **Journey of the Magi.** A six-month-long pilgrimage of peace will begin on January 6, 1999, to commemorate the bimillennial (two thousand years) era. The journey, on horses and camels, will retrace the original journey of the Magi through the Middle East and will end in Bethlehem with a twelve-day cultural festival for 10,000 participants. Other festivals will be held in cities along the journey route.
* **World Millennium Balls.** The ship *Queen Elizabeth II* will leave New York for a ten-day "Symposium at Sea." The ship's passengers will then travel to the Great Pyramid of Cheops in Egypt for a World Millennium Charity Ball on December 31, 1999. In addition, similar charity "celebrations of civilization" will be held at twenty-three locations around the world, including the Great Wall of China, the Taj Mahal in India, the Acropolis in Greece, and the Eiffel Tower in France.
* **March of the Millennium.** In honor of the two thousandth anniversary of the birth of Christ, more than 30 million people will participate in a global "March for Jesus" celebration on June 10, 2000. People in

more than two thousand cities around the world are expected to participate in this procession of prayer and worship.

* **Expo 2000.** Hanover, Germany, will be the site of the World's Fair in the year 2000. From June 1 to October 31, Expo 2000 will explore the state of the world through the theme "Mankind, Nature, and Technology." Approximately 40 million people are expected to visit.
* **Meta-Nation 2000.** United Societies in Space is a citizen's group devoted to the establishment of a meta-nation in space where human society can live and work in the new millennium. Toward that goal, a constitutional convention of 80,000 participants will meet in Denver's Mile High Stadium from August 2 through August 4, 2000, to form a space governance entity that can legally pave the way for private investment in their venture over the next century.
* **Olympics 2000.** The Games of the XXVII Olympiad will be held in Sydney, Australia, from September 16 through October 1. More than 10,000 athletes from 171 nations are expected to compete in the games.
* **Earth Day 2000.** Organizers of this event are expecting the largest Earth Day event ever for the year 2000. On April 22, more than 300 million people in 150 nations will participate in a celebration of the earth.

Chapter 2

Is It the End of the World?

Why do some people believe that the world will end in the year 2000?

For most people, the first day of January 2000 will be a time of great celebration, of looking back on past achievements and forward to the promise of the future. But with the end of any long period of time, it is natural also to feel a sense of dread. What if the end of a thousand years also signals the end of all time?

If the approach of the end of a century always brings an increased sense of anxiety among the people of the world, the end of a millennium is bound to produce even more fear and dread. This sense of dread is intensified by the fact that the process of change has accelerated incredibly in the twentieth century compared with previous centuries. This century has seen many more inventions, technological wonders, medical miracles, and other great changes than any other period of time. People who were born at midcentury, for example, have seen the computer revolution change the very way we live and work. These kinds of changes may be for the good, but they sometimes make us feel as if life is out of control.

Communications have made it possible for us to witness and hear about the many wars, famines, and disasters occurring throughout the world. Sometimes it seems as though the human race has never been in worse shape. We hear and read about overpopulation, disease, political unrest, and violence every day in newspapers, on television, and now on the Internet. It seems only natural to wonder: Are we hurtling toward some definite, terrible end to it all? And wouldn't it make sense for a great disaster to fall on the day that marks the end of a very long era? These fears persist even though, as we have seen, the year 2000 is technically only another day on the calendar.

The historian Hillel Schwartz has noted seven tendencies that take hold at the end of centuries—tendencies that are exaggerated at the end of a millennium. Among those that may explain why people feel a sense of doom are a tendency to:

Feel distress and depletion. Schwartz says that many people feel that we are living in an exhausted era, when traditions are disappearing. This tendency is increased by the sense that we are depleting the earth's energy and natural resources.

Get confused about conclusions. As Schwartz explains, "Centuries' ends seem [to go on forever]; the end has been held in sight for so long that it seems to take forever for anything decisive to happen. The desire for things to come to a head *soon* leads people to be jumpy: to jump to conclusions, to reverse themselves, to suppress the logic behind major decisions. . . ."

Go for broke. People feel that "events and inventions are spinning out of control," says Schwartz. Thus, many people begin to feel at this time that everything must be stopped—or fixed—now or never.

Many prophets and seers have appeared over the past twenty years or so exaggerating these fears, playing on the natural worries of people and claiming that the world will end. There are all kinds of people predicting the end of the world. Some are religious evangelists, some are New Age prophets, some are psychics, and some even claim to be messengers from outer space. Interpreting passages from the Bible and other works, they claim that all of the signs point to a major, violent change to come within the next few years. In addition, the prophecies of psychics and seers both past and present—which we will examine in the next chapter—are being brought up and reexamined for proof that the year 2000 will signal the end of the world.

To make the problem even more complicated, many people believe that the millennial year 2000 and the millennium of biblical prophecy—the period during which Christ will reign on earth for a thousand years—are the same thing. We will examine this question next.

Is the year 2000 the start of the promised millennium in biblical prophecy?

There is no necessary connection between the calendar's turn of the millennium and the one mentioned in the Bible, but many people find that the similarity in names makes it impossible not to connect the two. The year 2000 marks the third millennium of the Gregorian calendar, which is the calendar most people throughout the world follow and the one we discussed in the previous chapter. The millennium mentioned in the Bible comes from Revelation, the final book of the New Testament. It refers to the thousand-year period during which Jesus Christ will return and establish his kingdom on the earth, before the Last Judgment.

Our tendency to think of large units of time in terms of thousand-year cycles almost certainly comes from the many passages in the Bible that refer to a thousand years, including the reference in Revelation. However, only some people connect the new millennium to the one in Revelation. Some Christian groups assume that the year 2000 A.D. will be the beginning of the biblical millennium as well.

How did they arrive at this conclusion? Some base this belief on a biblical passage, II Peter 3:8, which says that, "with the Lord one day is as a thousand years." According to this calculation, if a thousand years is one day, then the seven days of creation described in Genesis symbolize the seven millennia of the world's history. The history of the world will unfold for six thousand years, after which earthly time will end and the millennium will begin. If, as one seventeenth-century biblical expert calculated, the world began around 4000 B.C., then the year 2000 marks the beginning of this seventh millennium, equivalent to the Lord's seventh day, the Sabbath day or day of rest—the beginning of Christ's reign on earth.

However, it is easy to see that we arrive at this calculation by only guessing at the date of the beginning of the world, a date most scientists say was about 3.5 billion years ago. The choice of 4000 B.C. is based on the chronologies of the Hebrew Old Testament, which were calculated by an Anglican archbishop named James Ussher in 1650. In fact, he set the moment of creation at exactly 4004 B.C., which would mean, technically, that the actual date of the seventh millennium has already occurred—in 1997. In fact, from early times, people have manipulated or guessed at the age of the world in order to say that the end of the world is coming on a specific day.

Still, the connection between the coming millennium and the millennial era described in Revelation holds a strong attraction for many Christians. The desire to match God's calendar with humankind's is an age-old occupation. In fact, the term *millenarian* is used to describe Christians who, throughout history, have believed that the millennium in the Bible is near. We will find out more about them in chapter 5.

Are there any biblical prophecies that predict the end of the world in the year 2000?

There is actually no place in the Bible that predicts the end of the world in the year 2000. Nor are there any signs recorded in the Bible that we can use to determine the exact date of Christ's return and the end of time. In fact, there are many passages, particularly in the Gospel according to Matthew, that emphasize that the time and place for the Second Coming of the Lord will be known to no one. Here are several of these passages:

> "But of that day and hour no one knows, not even the angels of heaven, nor the Son, but the Father only." (Matthew 24:36)
>
> "Therefore you also must be ready; for the Son of man is coming at an hour you do not expect." (Matthew 24:44)
>
> "Watch therefore, for you know neither the day nor the hour." (Matthew 25:13)

All the Bible tells us about the end of time is that the resurrection of the dead will occur at the time of Christ's return. Several verses record Jesus' statements that the resurrection will occur on the "last day":

"This is the will of My Father, that everyone who sees the Son and believes in Him should have eternal life; and I will raise him up at the last day." (John 6:40)

There is no indication, however, when that last day will be.

Before the birth of Jesus, did people believe that the end of the world was near?

Yes. In fact, starting around two hundred years before the birth of Jesus, there were many Jews and Romans who began to have visions of the end of time. Perhaps one of the most famous of these visions is recorded in the Book of Daniel in the Hebrew Bible. The Book of Daniel was written around 168 B.C., during the time that the Greek Seleucids were occupying Jerusalem. It was a very hard time for the Jewish people, and probably the writer of Daniel was attempting to lend courage to his people in their struggle against the Seleucids.

In the book, Daniel, a young Jewish boy, is called upon to explain a dream of King Nebuchadnezzar. In the dream, a great statue, made of gold, silver, bronze, iron, and clay, appears. The statue is shattered by a stone, which becomes a huge mountain and fills the earth. Daniel interprets the different materials of the statue as four evil kingdoms and the stone as a fifth kingdom, the kingdom of God on earth. After a series of great struggles among the kingdoms, a cataclysmic battle occurs in which a great tyrant is destroyed. Then a prince named Michael appears and brings with him "a time of trouble, such as never has been since there was a nation till that time; but at that time your people shall be delivered, every one whose name shall be found written in the book. And many of those who sleep in the dust of the earth shall awake, some to everlasting life, and some to shame and everlasting contempt. And those who are wise shall shine like the brightness of the firmament; and those who turn many to righteousness, like the stars for ever and ever" (Daniel 12:1-3).

At the time Daniel was written, many people believed that the great battle would come soon, that the Jews would conquer their enemies the Greeks, and that the great Judgment Day described in the passage above—when both the living and the dead of the Jewish people would be united in a new world order—was just around the corner. The Book of Daniel demonstrates that the idea of a world-ending catastrophic battle was alive in the minds of many Jews at that time. Later, Christians would point to the Book of Daniel as a prophecy of the coming of Christ. Today, some Christians see it as foretelling the end of the world, which will occur when the next millennium arrives.

Similarly, many Romans in the first century before the birth of Christ became convinced that Rome would be destroyed during "the Great Year," which they believed was coming soon. The Great Year, according to Roman myth, could be calculated according to a mystic number revealed to Romulus, the founder of Rome, by twelve eagles. Whenever a crisis in the Roman Empire occurred, the number was calculated to match the year of the crisis. Any catastrophes at the time were pointed to as evidence that the end was near.

What are some groups in our own time that have believed the world will end?

Because of the approaching millennium, there are probably more groups today that believe the end is near than there have ever been in history. We will see some of the more famous of these prophets and their followers in chapters 3 and 6: the Branch Davidians, who died in a confrontation with the FBI in April 1993; the Aum Shinrikyo group in Japan, which was responsible for the sarin gas attack in Toyoko; and the Heaven's Gate cult, whose members committed group suicide in San Diego in 1997. All of these groups believed that the world's destruction is approaching with the new millennium. But there have been countless lesser-known groups and cults in the second half of the twentieth century that have predicted and awaited the end of the world.

The Branch Davidians of Waco, Texas, fame, for example, were preceded by another group of the same name. This earlier group was founded in the 1930s by a man named Victor Houteff, a washing machine salesman who was convinced that the terrors of the final reckoning and the return of Christ were at hand. He started a community in Waco (near the site of the community of the later Davidians), where a clock was set permanently at 11:00 P.M. to remind his followers that time was coming to an end. Houteff died in 1955, but his widow prophesied in a radio broadcast that the day of reckoning would occur on a specific date. On this day, the faithful would be killed and their bodies carried to heaven. Accordingly, hundreds of Houteff's followers gathered at his widow's house on April 22, 1959, the appointed day. Nothing happened, and all of the followers went home.

Another group that prophesied the end of the world—again and again—was the Bahá'ís Under the Provisions of the Covenant (BUPC), a group that broke away from the Bahá'í faith in the 1970s. The leader of this group, Leland Jensen, first predicted the end of the world on April 29, 1980. The BUPC built fallout shelters to wait out the nuclear holocaust that would occur that day, taking a third of the world's population with it. Afterward, they believed, famine and revolution would reign for twenty years, until God's kingdom on earth would be established in the year 2000.

When this prophecy failed to come true, Jensen predicted that Halley's comet would crash into the earth in 1986, bringing on many natural disasters that would end in a great battle between the forces of good and evil. This, too, failed to happen. After a number of similar predictions also failed to come true, Jensen predicted that a nuclear bomb would destroy New York City on March 23, 1994, bringing on the Battle of Armageddon forty days later, during which a third of humanity would be killed in one hour. After this failed prediction, many of Jensen's followers finally became disillusioned and left the group.

Some religious groups have learned their lessons from failed prophecies like these. For example, the Jehovah's Witnesses have predicted that the world would end on a specific day almost a dozen times in the past hundred years. After seeing so many prophecies fail, they now refuse to make predictions. Still, their spokesman, Robert Johnson, insists that the end is near. He just doesn't want to say exactly when that will be. "The Bible has a list of about two dozen things to watch out for," Johnson says. "They've all happened."

Many people have heard of the phenomenon of the "rapture," a term some fundamentalist Christian groups use to describe the moment when the world will end and faithful souls will be transported up to heaven immediately, no matter where they are or what they are doing. Perhaps you have seen bumper stickers that say "This vehicle will be unoccupied in case of rapture," which means beware, because the driver will suddenly vanish up to heaven when Judgment Day arrives, leaving behind an unmanned automobile. In the 1980s, a man named Edgar Whisenant published a booklet called *88 Reasons Why the Rapture Will Be in 1988*. Using interpretations based on the Book of Daniel and Revelation, among others, Whisenant claimed that the "rapture" would occur on October 3, 1988. Again, when the prediction failed to come true, he moved the date of the end of the world to one year later, in 1989. As we know, that prophecy failed to come true as well.

A pair of prophets—appropriately named Mark and Elizabeth Clare Prophet—claimed to be in contact with Jesus Christ, Buddha, and Confucius, among other wise men. They predicted, based on astrological calculations, that the world would be destroyed in a great cataclysm in 1990. Elizabeth Prophet commanded her followers to sell their property and move to a large ranch in Montana to await the end. The end did not come.

In 1998, a prophet from Taiwan who had moved with his followers to Garland, Texas, predicted that God would appear on channel 18 of every television set in the world on March 25. This prophet, Heng-ming Chen, claimed that six days after God's television appearance, he would appear at Chen's residence and take human form in Chen's body. This event would lead up to the destruction of Asia by nuclear war in 1999. When God failed to make the scheduled TV appearance, Chen claimed that people would begin seeing God in their dreams in the form of Chen's body. Chen offered to allow his followers to kill him if this prophecy did not come true. So far, Chen is still alive and has moved his followers to Lake Michigan to await flying saucers, which will take them away when the nuclear holocaust occurs.

These are only a few random examples of prophets who have recently predicted the end of the world. It is impossible to know how many more there are right now, but it's probable that there are many. The *Millennial Prophecy Report* follows the activities of 1,100 different groups and individuals in America that have ideas about the approaching end of the world. And with the possibilities for global, instant communication offered by the Internet, it is probable that the number of those who predict doom and gloom to come will grow even greater before the year 2000.

What happens when end-of-the-world prophecies don't come true?

So far, anyone who has believed fervently that a certain date would bring the end of the world has obviously been disappointed. The reactions of those who have experienced this disappointment are varied. For prophets who predict the end of the world, one response has often been to simply move the date of the End Time to some point farther in the future. Another way prophets justify their failure is to point to some event that occurred on or around the prophetic date as proof that "something" happened. For example, when Leland Jensen, the leader of the BUPC, realized that his prediction of a bomb destroying New York City had not come true, he quickly pointed out that a gas pipeline had exploded in New Jersey the very next day.

The explosion had "fulfilled" the prophecy, even if it hadn't brought about the end of the world.

For the followers who believe in such prophecies, however, these explanations and justifications often cannot overcome the disappointment and disillusionment that comes with a failed prediction. Sometimes the followers disband and pretend that the incident never happened. Some latch on to another prophecy or belief and commit themselves to it just as deeply, if not more deeply. Unfortunately, some believers—such as the Heaven's Gate cult, as we will see—have such faith in the prediction that they give their lives in the belief that it will come true.

Why do people believe in end-of-the-world prophecies?

There are probably as many reasons people believe in such predictions as there are prophets of doom. One rather far-fetched philosopher has even explained the belief in the end of the world as a way to compensate for the fact that we never got to see its beginning—the Big Bang, as scientists call the creation of the world. In other words, since we missed the beginning, at least we can look forward to being around at the end!

Of course, we all believe that the world will end someday—many millions of years in the future. Most scientists agree that as far as they are able to tell, the end of the world is a very, very long way off. And most of us probably are not eager to see the world and everyone in it perish. But those who do believe the world will soon end usually don't believe that they themselves will die. Rather, most end-of-the-world prophecies predict the *end of the world as it is*. People and places may be destroyed, but the faithful will live or be resurrected to create a new order, perhaps on a transformed earth or perhaps in heaven. In this newly made world, peace, harmony and justice will reign, and there will be no suffering.

While most people would like to see a world like this, those who believe in doomsday prophecies think that life as we know it will end very soon, very suddenly, and—usually—very violently, in order to create the new paradise. Before the "day of reckoning," these people completely devote themselves to preparing for it—building special bunkers or shelters, isolating themselves from former friends and family, leaving behind old possessions. The prophet they follow—often someone with very persuasive powers—may make them feel that to leave the group is very risky. If they leave, they will not be among the chosen few who will survive the final disaster.

The idea of being transported to a better world can be appealing to those who feel that too many things are changing too quickly or that the world seems to be in crisis. In such a world, we can understand the appeal of feeling that all of it will come to a sudden end, as will our problems and conflicts. Also, the belief in a world that will end soon makes everything in the present take on new meaning. If we believe that a great destiny is about to be fulfilled that only we know about, our lives are suddenly filled with a sense of purpose and urgency. Everyday occurrences are no longer important, but preparing for the Great Event suddenly makes our individual lives seem very important.

Many people who have survived doomsday cults describe the feeling that they belonged to a unique, closed society with special knowledge about the future that the rest of the world either ignores or scorns. Belief in a catastrophic end of the world was a way of giving their lives meaning, a way of making them feel more powerful in a world they felt powerless to change.

Again, those who believe the world will soon end usually see a better world to come, a world in which they will be protected from evil and the violence of the final battle. For those who look around in the late twentieth century and see only the many troubles that surround us, such a belief seems very comforting.

What are some scary ideas today about what will happen in the year 2000?

Many prophecies for the year 2000 center around the return of Christ, which will in turn be preceded or followed by events such as a nuclear holocaust, famine, earthquakes, and/or violent, all-encompassing wars among nations. In addition to these kinds of prophecies, many seers have predicted nothing more or less than great geological changes that will have devastating effects on the earth.

A book by Jeffrey Goodman called *The Earthquake Generation* contains a list of some of the geological changes that a number of psychics agree will occur in the world around the year 2000. For example:

* There will be a major shift of the polar axis.
* There will be major disturbances on both coasts of the United States.
* Major sections of the United States will fall into the sea, and a final coastline will be established in Nebraska.
* Large parts of Texas and Florida will be completely underwater.
* Parts of the British Isles will submerge, while others will rise.
* London will be a coastal town.

* Most of Hawaii and Japan will break apart.
* There will be major earthquakes in Turkey and Yugoslavia.

Some of these forewarnings are combined in the prophecies of a contemporary seer, Ruth Montgomery. She predicts that in the summer or autumn of 1999, the earth will turn over on its side. This will result in a shifting of the North and South Poles to South America and the Pacific Ocean. The dramatic movement of the earth's axis will cause oceans to engulf land masses in giant tidal waves. California, the British Isles, the Netherlands, and Japan will be submerged; hurricanes will occur everywhere around the globe.

Montgomery believes, however, that there will be a small number of people who will survive these catastrophes by moving to high ground. They will be helped by others who will have been spirited to safety by extraterrestrials—beings from outer space. After the cataclysm, the aliens, in turn, will "return to designated areas," claims Montgomery, "soothing and reassuring [survivors] and teaching them new methods of growing crops more speedily and... erecting dwellings that require little time or energy." Those who are not capable of living in this new world will die off after a time.

Montgomery is one of a number of seers who predict the coming of the Antichrist at the approach of the millennium. Apparently, this Antichrist may already be among us. Montgomery claims that "he has already been born and is now an American boy in his early teens." The famous fashion designer and current New Age guru Paco Rabanne says that there is currently a man in his late twenties living in London "who has surprised important people with his 'magic' gifts." Perhaps, Rabanne says, he is the Antichrist awaiting his time to appear. When that time comes, likely at the end of 1990s, he will lead the forces of evil in the final battle of the End Time. As we will see in the next chapter, a few more famous seers also have predicted an appearance by the Antichrist at the end of the millennium.

Another doomsday scenario revolves around the Great Planetary Cross of 1999, which will occur shortly after the last total solar eclipse of the century on August 11, 1999. The planets will be aligned in a way that some astrologers predict will bring about violent and destructive earthquakes. Most astronomers agree, though, that this event will have very little, if any, effect on the earth.

In sum, just about any kind of major catastrophe we can imagine has been predicted by someone somewhere for the turn of the millennium. It is wise, however, to remember all of the countless prophecies by people who have claimed the end of the world was at hand on a certain date. So far, none of these prophecies has come true.

Does anyone think good things will happen in the year 2000?

Despite all of the prophecies of terrible events, most people are not anticipating anything special to happen in the year 2000. At the same time, many people believe that the turning of the new millennium will bring about a new era in which wonderful things will happen.

The same Great Planetary Cross that for some prophets spells disaster will for others signal the beginning of the Age of Aquarius, a time of enlightenment and peace that was mentioned in a popular song of the 1960s. This New Age (from which the New Age movement gets its name) will mean the passing of the Piscean Age, to be replaced by the sign of Aquarius, whose values are those of friendship, peace, and community.

As James Manning notes in his book *Prophecies for the New Millennium*, one of the champions of this New Age is a Native American "spirit guide" named Silver Birch, who speaks through a medium. Birch claims that the new millennium will "mean the end of separateness between peoples. It will mean the end of national barriers, race distinctions, class distinctions, color distinctions, and all the distinctions between churches and chapels, temples, mosques, and synagogues. . . . Out of apparent confusion, the divine pattern will take shape, harmony and peace will come."

Many other groups and individuals are hoping to use the excitement and energy created by the turn of the new millennium to make something good happen. Along with the many celebrations mentioned in chapter 1, practically every major city in the world will hold special events and gatherings during the millennium, celebrating the opportunity to look forward to the future and to create ways to improve the quality of life. In addition, special organizations have been formed to promote goodwill and positive change.

For example, the World Peace 2000 Network, a group based in New Jersey, is planning an "International Day of Peace in 2000" during which governments and individuals will agree to lay down their weapons for a single day and issue a proclamation of peace. The group is calling its efforts the World Peace Movement. One of the founders of the World Peace 2000 Network has said, "It is going to be a turning point for humanity. We are hoping to ride this incredible wave of emotion and spread a message of world peace into the next century." So far, the group has gained the support of twenty-one world leaders and is currently awaiting word from the president of the United States to see if he will endorse the project.

Jay Gary, a Baptist minister from Colorado Springs, Colorado, is using the millennium as an opportunity to encourage people to express and realize their dreams. He is the moderator of an Internet-based discussion group called Talk 2000, in which people debate and set goals for the year 2000. In this way, people of differing beliefs and ideas can communicate and effect positive change. Gary sees the millennium not only as a chance to honor the two thousandth anniversary of the birth of Jesus but also as an opportunity to celebrate human aspirations. His book, *The Star of 2000: Our Journey toward Hope*, is in part about how different people have approached the year 2000 in the past thirty years.

In short, there are many people in the world who, rather than approaching the next millennium with a sense of doom, see themselves as extremely lucky to be among the very few in history to experience this extraordinary event. For them, the year 2000 is not a world-ending threat but the promise of a new beginning.

Chapter 3

What Do the Prophets and Seers Say?

There have been so many prophecies throughout the ages about the year 2000 that it is impossible to account for all of them, or even most of them. As the time of the third millennium approaches, new prophets and seers seem to be appearing almost every day. This chapter includes the millennial prophecies of some of the more famous seers in history, as well as current prophecies about the year 2000 that have sprung up over the past few years. Most of them predict some kind of catastrophe—even the end of the world—for the new millennium, although a few predict more hopeful events.

Saint Malachy

One of the earliest predictions that people use to forecast the end of the world is a list of popes written by Saint Malachy of Ireland. Saint Malachy, who was born in 1094, became a priest at the age of twenty-five and later was made a bishop. In 1190, forty-two years after his death, he became the first Irishman to be canonized.

In 1139, Saint Malachy presented his list to Pope Innocent II. It predicted all future popes through Peter of Rome, during whose papacy the Last Judgment would occur:

> During the last persecution of the Holy Roman Church, there shall sit Petrus Romanus [Peter of Rome], who shall feed the sheep amid great Tribulations, and when these have passed, the City of the Seven Hills shall be utterly destroyed, and the awful Judge will judge the people.

However, Saint Malachy's list was not discovered until 1595, and some people consider it a fake. First, it reappeared at a time when the papacy was undergoing hard times, and the list conveniently provided proof that the papacy would survive. Second, the list is very specific about all of the popes up until 1590 and then grows increasingly vague about exactly who would be pope after that.

Nevertheless, the list is being reexamined today because it names only two more popes after the current one, Pope John Paul II. Some people say that John Paul II, who is in frail health, could die at any time. Perhaps another pope who also could die soon would replace him. That would mean that the final pope on Saint Malachy's list could be sitting on the papal throne in the year 2000, in time for the Last Judgment.

Nostradamus

Perhaps no seer's predictions have been so famous or had such lasting popularity as those of the French prophet Nostradamus. Born in 1503, Nostradamus was a highly educated doctor and mathematician who also was fascinated by astrology. By the time he was thirty, he was working as a doctor and became famous in his own time for fighting the plague, which was then raging throughout Europe.

Nostradamus believed himself to be descended from one of the ten lost tribes of Israel, a tribe that was reputed to have prophetic gifts. As a young man, he often angered his religious teachers because he openly defended astrology and was interested in alchemy and other mystical arts.

But Nostradamus's prophetic gifts did not reach full flower until after the tragic deaths of his young wife and two children during the plague. That's when he started to record in an almanac the prophecies that began coming to him. Soon he felt a calling to undertake a great project: a future history of the world, to be set down in a series of quatrains—four-line stanzas. He grouped the quatrains in collections called *Centuries*, so called because they were meant to contain 100 verses each. In fact, the ten *Centuries* contain 942 quatrains altogether.

Nostradamus began writing his ten books of prophecies on the evening of Good Friday in 1554. Because he wanted to avoid being called a magician or witch—very dangerous charges in his day—he wrote his prophecies out of chronological order. To further confuse any accusers, he wrote in a mixture of languages, symbols, anagrams, metaphors, and grammatical tricks.

Because of this, the quatrains are often difficult to interpret. And many of Nostradamus's predictions in *Centuries* have been interpreted in many different ways throughout the 430 years since his death. Often he used anagrams of names instead of actual names in his predictions. It is said that Nostradamus accurately predicted the rise of Hitler, for example, because he mentions an evil leader named Hister in one of them. Still, many of the quatrains are much more vague than that and can be applied to a wide range of events that have happened or are about to happen.

Now that the millennium is approaching, there is a renewed interest in Nostradamus's prophecies, since many of them seem to refer to the end of the twentieth century. He referred to the coming of "a very evil century," which many people assume must refer to our own. He is said to have predicted the Gulf War in 1991, the end of the Soviet Union in the mid-1990s, and the spread of AIDS throughout the world in the past twenty years. But the quatrain that has given rise to the most interest lately is also the one where Nostradamus was uncharacteristically specific about a particular date:

> In the year 1999 and seven months,
> From the skies shall come a great king of terror.
> To bring back to life the Great King of the Moguls,
> Before and after Mars reigns happily. (*Century* 10, 72)

From this quatrain, many people have predicted that there will be some kind of world-ending catastrophe in July 1999, although there are all kinds of different ideas about who the "king of terror" and the "Great King of the Moguls" might be. Some say the king of terror may be the third Antichrist (Napoleon and Hitler being the first two) named Mabus that Nostradamus predicted in another quatrain. However, Nostradamus also predicted that after the terrible event of terror in 1999, a long period of peace would follow. The quatrain that follows the prediction of the king of terror is more optimistic but just as confusing:

> All things shall be set into a new order of the ages,
> The new century and millennium will see an opening to
> a new way,
> Those who have hidden behind masks of lofty power
> will be changed
> Few will be found who shall remain in leadership.

Nostradamus's predictions, in fact, go as far as 3997 A.D., which he apparently believed would be the actual year of the end of the world. So his prediction about July 1999 cannot be a prophecy of the total end of the world in the year 2000.

Helena Petrovna Blavatsky

Helena Petrovna Blavatsky was a Russian spiritualist who was born in 1831 and who founded the Theosophical Society in the 1870s. The Theosophical Society, which still exists, believes that all world religions eventually will merge into one great religion.

At seventeen, Blavatsky married a man of forty. She later ran away from him. There followed a period in which she claimed, among other things, to have ridden bareback in the circus, toured Serbia as a concert pianist, and traveled alone in Tibet for seven years. While in Tibet, she developed a passion for the mysticism and religions of the East. Afterward, she came to America, where she wrote and published a series of letters that she claimed were being dictated to her by the spirits of religious masters in India and Tibet and that are still in print today. The basic idea behind these writings is that a divine reality lies behind all ideas and religions, that all religions will eventually be united into one, and that only those of a loving and pure heart can see the divine reality.

Although Blavatsky wrote no specific predictions for the year 2000, she did prophesy that in the year 1975 there would be a rapid spread of Eastern religions in the West. The old religions of the West would slowly die, and in subsequent years leading up to the new millennium a new race of people would be formed. They would be spiritually superior to those who came before them and would be able to see the divine reality. The birthplace of this new race of people would be America:

> . . . Even now, under our very eyes, the new Race and races are preparing to be formed, and that it is in America that the transformation will take place. Thus it is the mankind of the New World, whose mission and Karma it is to sow the seeds for a forthcoming grander and far more glorious Race than any of those we know of at present. (*The Secret Doctrine*, 1888)

Could it be that Blavatsky predicted the growing interest in Eastern religions that began in the 1970s and continues today? Strangely enough, Nostradamus also claimed that Christian ideals would be replaced by Eastern philosophies as the year 2000 approached.

Blavatsky also is said to have predicted the coming of a current New Age prophet named The Lord Maitreya. In her book *Isis Unveiled*, which she claimed was written by three Tibetan Masters, one of the Masters told Blavatsky that The Lord Maitreya would appear at the dawn of the Age of Aquarius, which takes place at the end of this millennium. In 1977, a Himalayan spiritual leader called The Lord Maitreya went to live in London. From there, he has issued guidelines for humankind's salvation through a spokesperson. The Lord Maitreya warns that people everywhere must be provided with food, housing, and education and that world tensions must be resolved. Otherwise, he predicts, World War III will usher in the end of the world.

Edgar Cayce

Edgar Cayce, one of the twentieth century's most famous prophets, made major and specific predictions about the millennium. Born on a farm in Kentucky in 1877, Cayce discovered his ability to see and talk to visions at the age of six. He was called America's Sleeping Prophet because he would lie down on a couch and, from a trancelike state, prescribe medical cures for the sick.

In addition to his healing powers, Cayce saw thousands of visions of the future. He called the being that gave him his visions The Universal Mind. During the 1930s, Cayce received numerous visions of a coming world war in which millions of people would be killed. He is said to have given many accurate dates and descriptions of the time and length of World War II.

Today, many people point to Cayce's millennial prophecies as proof that the world will soon end. Under the influence of the Universal Mind, Cayce predicted the destruction of many parts of the world by 1998, the beginning of World War III in 1999, and the end of civilization as we know it in the year 2000. Cayce predicted that he himself would be reincarnated in Nebraska in 2100, a survivor of the end of the world. He saw himself returning to America in a cigar-shaped aircraft from which he would view the total devastation of the country. He would land in the ruins of a former city and ask, "Where am I?" "New York City" would be the reply.

Cayce predicted a series of earth-shattering events leading up to the year 2000. Between 1988 and 1998, he prophesied, wide-scale destruction would come to Los Angeles, San Francisco, and New York. In the late 1990s, floods would cover the Midwest and Northeast, and New York City, South Carolina, and Georgia would be underwater. A "ring of fire" would encompass Japan, China, Southeast Asia, Australia, and South America, and Japan itself would fall into the sea. The North and South Poles would shift positions and Europe would undergo severe temperature changes. Major geological shifts would herald a new cycle of humankind. All of this would happen by 1998. In 1999, World War III would begin.

Despite all of these prophecies of doom, Cayce believed that this worldwide destruction would eventually lead to the creation of a New Jerusalem and a time of spiritual renewal. Perhaps he himself would see this time of rebirth in his reincarnated self. Cayce once predicted that a child named John Penniel would be born in America and grow up to be "beloved of all men in all places, when the universality of God in the earth has been proclaimed. He will come as a messenger not a forerunner, and give to the earth a new order of things." This child would come to recognition at a time of "several major earth changes." Perhaps in the year 2000?

Jeane Dixon

Jeane Dixon, who died in 1997 at seventy-nine, was one of the most famous psychics of our time. She first became well known when she predicted the assassination of President John F. Kennedy. Today, many people are reexamining her prophecy that a savior of humankind will appear before the year 2000 and turn into the Antichrist.

On February 5, 1962, Dixon looked out her bedroom window in Washington, D.C., and saw a vision of a desert at sunrise. There, a huge crowd surrounded Queen Nefertiti and the Pharaoh Akhenaton of ancient Egypt. Nefertiti presented the people with a newborn baby who suddenly grew into a man. The crowd, Dixon realized, was composed of all members of the human race, and all of them were kneeling before the man. Dixon interpreted her vision to mean that a great leader had been born who would unify the whole world and that the true meaning of the vision would not be revealed until 1999. A few years later, Dixon announced that she had been wrong about a crucial point in the vision: The man was not a great, humane leader but the Antichrist who would rule the world from Jerusalem.

Hal Lindsey

In 1973, Christian evangelist Hal Lindsey wrote a book that quickly became one of the most popular nonfiction books in history. The book, *Late Great Planet Earth*, became the single best-selling English-language book of the 1970s, selling more than a million copies. It rested its interpretation of the End Time on a reading of Revelation.

Lindsey identified the ten horns of the beast in Revelation 13 with the ten nations of the European Common Market. Lindsey claimed further that two then-current events foreshadowed the last days described elsewhere in Revelation: the dominance of China and the proposed creation of a pan-Arab union by the late Egyptian president Gamal Abdel Nasser. The "great harlot" described in Revelation was the National and World Councils of Churches, comprised of Methodist, Presbyterian, Baptist, Episcopalian, Lutheran, and other churches.

But none of these identifications was as powerful a proof of the approaching end of the world as the foundation of the State of Israel in 1948. According to Lindsey, the return of the Jews to the Holy Land touched off the very beginning of the End Time, and Lindsey claimed that there would be one generation between that event and Christ's Second Coming. A biblical generation is forty years, so Christ's return could be predicted for some time in the late 1980s or possibly up until the third millennium. Lindsey called the people living in this time after 1948 the Terminal Generation.

Dr. Billy Graham

Dr. Billy Graham, the world-renowned evangelist, has probably presented the words of the gospel to more people than anyone else in history. He has been a spiritual advisor to many presidents and world leaders and has written a number of best-selling books about faith and Christianity. In his 1983 book *Approaching Hoofbeats: The Four Horsemen of the Apocalypse*, Dr. Graham took on the role of a prophet to discuss the issues that he feels are a threat to our future and that may signal the end of the world if we do not change. Through an examination of the final book of the New Testament, Revelation, Dr. Graham predicts that many of the world's current ills may lead to Armageddon—the final battle between good and evil.

In Revelation, Dr. Graham finds a warning about the coming millennium that we must all heed in order to stave off disaster. He recalls the first six chapters of the book, in which the prophet John of Patmos (who wrote Revelation) warned of the four horses ridden by "the four horsemen of the Apocalypse." These horses represent four signs of coming disaster: "The *first horse* has to do with counterfeit religion. The *second* deals with war and peace. The *third* has to do with famine and pestilence. And the *fourth* represents the trauma of death and the sufferings of Hades."

The first horse, Dr. Graham explains, tells us to beware the danger of false religions, which are so common in today's society: cults and cult leaders, false faith healers, and the false god of material wealth, all of which lead away from belief in the one true God. The second horse warns of the danger of nuclear war, which Dr. Graham believes could destroy the world if the use of nuclear weapons is not curbed. The third horse signals the rising incidence of poverty and famine, which will lead to disaster unless those of us who have plenty help feed the sick and starving of the world. The fourth horseman warns us to make positive changes in our troubled world before it is too late. This fourth horseman is death, and Dr. Graham says that we must become actively involved in making the world a better place—including saving the earth from pollution and disease—in order to head off ultimate destruction.

In *Approaching Hoofbeats*, Dr. Graham is careful not to predict the exact time when the Day of Judgment will arrive. He notes that although many people expect the end of the world in the year 2000, the Bible instructs us that the time is not for us to know. But he does say that the Bible tells us that judgment will certainly come and that God will not put it off indefinitely. Perhaps the signs of disaster in our day are a warning to us that the day is approaching. For Dr. Graham, these signs are an indication that those who wish to be saved must accept Christ as their savior and work for social justice on this earth. Through good works and the acceptance of Christ, the terrible Day of Judgment may be postponed, and the new millennium can begin in hope instead of fear.

Pope John Paul II

The current leader of the Roman Catholic Church, Pope John Paul II, was elected in 1978. He has been preparing for the coming millennium for many years. In 1995, he issued a letter—*Tertio Millennio Adveniente*, or "The Coming of the Third Millennium"—explaining how Roman Catholics should prepare for the two thousandth anniversary of the birth of Christ. He also declared the year 2000 a Jubilee Year for the church, a time of special celebration and worship.

According to the pope's letter, all Catholics should begin a three-year preparation for the Jubilee Year. In 1997, that preparation consisted of contemplating Jesus and the mystery of salvation. In 1998, it consisted of thinking about the meaning of the Holy Spirit, which is believed to be the perfect force created from God's contemplation of his Son, Jesus. In 1999, Catholics were to undertake a contemplation of themselves, their sins, and their consciences.

Pope John Paul II has a very positive vision of the new millennium. Rather than predicting the end of the world, he sees the coming age as a time when the church will be revitalized. More and more people will rediscover their faith, and a new growth in spirituality will occur: "A new springtime of Christian life will be revealed by the Great Jubilee, if Christians are docile to the action of the Holy Spirit." He sees the fall of Communism, a new awareness of the environment, and a commitment to helping the poor as positive signs that the third millennium will be a sacred time of great hope for Christianity.

Previous popes, however, had less optimistic visions of the future. For example, Pope Pius X had a terrible vision in 1909 at a meeting with some Franciscan monks. He suddenly went into a trance and came out of it with a look of horror in his eyes. "What I have seen was terrible," he said. Sometime in the future, he claimed, a pope would "flee the Vatican and leave Rome. He will have to walk over the dead bodies of his priests."

Jeane Dixon once predicted that a pope would be assassinated before the year 2000, after which the Roman Catholic Church would split into various different groups of worshipers.

John Hogue

John Hogue, who lives in Seattle, Washington, is an authority on prophets. He has written two books about Nostradamus as well as *The Millennium Book of Prophecy*, a collection of 777 visions and predictions from a great many prophets and seers throughout history, including Nostradamus, Edgar Cayce, and numerous others. In this book, Hogue describes a car accident in which he was involved in 1981. Before the accident—during which he lost consciousness for twenty minutes but was unharmed—he had a premonition that something terrible was about to happen to him. Afterward, he determined to keep his mind open to the gift of premonition, and he believes that everyone should do likewise. His work on prophecy is an urgent attempt to spread word of the many predictions that he believes spell disaster for the coming millennium.

Accordingly, most of Hogue's interpretations of the prophecies of others are pretty grim. Again and again, he warns that various predictions from the past are a definite indication that the end of time will arrive between the years 2000 and 2012. Unless we take heed now and listen to the prophets, Hogue believes, we are destined for a terrible holocaust. For example, he says that Nostradamus predicted that "in the 1990s the earth will be engulfed in a nuclear Third World War ignited by a strong master of Islamic law who will wage a jihad [holy war] against the U.S., U.S.S.R. and Europe." This leader—whom Nostradamus called Mabus and who many people believe is Saddam Hussein—will fan the flames of Islamic fundamentalism into a global war, which will last three years and seven months and leave the earth covered with radioactive dust.

Hogue's interpretations of other prophets are similarly pessimistic. In fact, he believes that "the hazards now threatening human survival are more plentiful and severe than at any time in the earth's history. We may not make it through the dark waters of the next few decades. Even the finest prophetic surveyors cannot design a bridge for us to cross to the other shore." He does say, though, that our only hope is to abandon traditional ways of thinking, old ideas, and old religions. This involves embracing ideas that often are extreme and controversial. For example, Hogue says that genetic engineering is one step toward avoiding disaster, for it may remove criminal impulses from the human brain and disease and deformity from the human body. Such extreme measures may be necessary, Hogue believes, for the human race to survive the coming millennium.

Like many prophets of New Age thinking, Hogue maintains that a whole new, radically different way of thinking must be born in order to overcome the disasters ahead: "The next great age will only come for those who are ready to change, to drop those traditions of the dying [age] that no longer work to keep the human race growing in consciousness. . . . In the eleventh hour an "Apocalypse of Consciousness" will preclude a global death."

John Hagee

John Hagee is the pastor of the Cornerstone Church in San Antonio, Texas. A Christian Evangelist, Hagee is the author of *Beginning of the End: The Assassination of Yitzhak Rabin and the Coming Antichrist*. In his book, Hagee predicts that sometime soon, Islam will unite with a reborn Soviet Union to invade Israel. A global war will begin, and the Antichrist—whom Hagee says is already among us—will appear and set himself up as God. He will lead Israel into a fight with 200 million Chinese at Armageddon. Then Jesus will appear to defeat the forces of evil. After Christ reigns for a thousand years, God will destroy the world, and eternity will begin in heaven.

Because of Israel's essential place in fulfilling the prophesied events, Hagee urges Christians to support Israel and to defend the Jewish people against attack. The Jews have a biblical command to occupy the land of Israel and must be supported in their efforts to remain there. Hagee advises that the United States cannot survive the coming final battle unless it continues to help Israel. Hagee himself has helped to raise money for many Jewish causes and has aided in the effort to help Russian Jews immigrate to Israel. Hagee is not specific about when the coming End Time will arrive. But he believes that it will be soon and that the assassination of Israeli Premier Yitzhak Rabin was a sign that the end is near.

James Redfield

In 1996, James Redfield wrote a book that quickly became a best-seller and a media event. The insights and prophecies in the book have inspired countless discussion groups and Internet sites. *The Celestine Prophecy* is told in the form of a novel, but it is really a book of prophecy and a guide to the coming age, which Redfield believes will bring about a major change in the way humans think.

The plot of *The Celestine Prophecy* involves a nameless social worker who is undergoing a crisis in his career. He travels to Peru, where he finds an ancient prophetic manuscript that the Peruvian government and the Catholic Church want to keep from being known. The ancient manuscript contains the Nine Insights, each of which reveals some mystery or wisdom about the universe, human nature, and the evolution of humankind.

Through the characters and plot, *The Celestine Prophecy* explains Redfield's ideas about human destiny and its fulfillment through the Nine Insights. Redfield believes that the turmoil of the late twentieth century will give birth to a coming spiritual awakening, if only we follow the wisdom of the Nine Insights. These insights teach us that the universe is made up of energy, which is evolving into ever-higher forms of vibration. The final stage of this evolution will come when humans begin to direct that energy toward connecting with nature and their fellow humans rather than toward conflict with each other. Redfield believes that the past fifty years have been a preparation for this final stage.

To evolve to a higher state of being, we must follow the advice of the Nine Insights. A number of these involve letting go of childhood hurts and conflicts, learning to become less attached to material things, and learning to love each other and our planet. Competition and conflict with others must cease, for it only takes up energy that can be used for more positive emotions. Finally, the Ninth Insight promises a vision of fulfillment and peace:

> Our purpose here is to evolve consciously. As our planet evolves through greater technology we are freed up to spend more time to evolve spiritually. As we spend more time connecting with our Higher Source we experience a higher vibratory energy which nurtures each other, our planet, and ourselves. We eventually connect with God's energy in such a way that we become beings of light and the kingdom of heaven is manifested here on earth.

Unlike many other prophets, Redfield sees a bright future ahead for humankind. The world will not end but will be transformed by spiritual evolution through the Nine Insights.

Marshall T. Savage

In 1988, space engineer Marshall T. Savage founded the First Millennial Foundation, a Colorado-based organization devoted to promoting the colonization of space. Savage believes that because of overpopulation, the earth is poised on the brink of disaster, a "watershed of Cosmic history." If the population explosion continues, only nuclear war, plague, or famine will prevent total extinction in the next few decades—and all of these are horrible scenarios. Therefore, our only chance for survival in the next millennium is to eventually build a new civilization on Mars.

Savage's book, *Millennial Project*, was published in 1995 and lays out his plan to colonize the galaxy in eight steps. As he does not believe there is life on other planets, he sees the entire galaxy as being empty and at our disposal. The first step in Savage's plan is to colonize the ocean surface with floating cities, increasing the earth's living space and shifting its source of energy to the thermal energy of the deep ocean. This, in turn, will free up energy and resources to invent more efficient space vehicles for orbiting space colonies and settlements on the moon. The next step involves creating an atmosphere and water supply on Mars to form another earth-like planet. On an even longer time line, humans will expand into the entire solar system. With so much solar energy at our command, we can eventually send out whole populations to other stars. At the beginning of the fourth millennium, Savage predicts, there will be human colonies as far as forty or fifty light-years away.

In *Millennial Project*, Savage combines prophecy with science. Like many prophets, he predicts that the end of the world is coming soon. But unlike many of the prophets we have seen, he proposes a solution that calls on human rather than divine intervention. In fact, although most scientists believe that his plan for the future is far-fetched, many agree that some of his ideas are based on solid science and are well worth exploring.

The Gaia Movement

The Gaia Movement is an environmental organization devoted to promoting awareness of dangers to the earth's ecology. *Gaia* is the Greek name for the goddess of the earth. The movement keeps track of environmental events concerning geology, weather, the oceans, and natural disasters on the eve of the millennium. Gaians predict that unless serious action is taken, environmental disaster will destroy the earth in the next few years. The purpose of the Gaia Movement is to unite people everywhere in stopping the destruction of the earth to avert what Gaians see as inevitable disaster through irresponsible management of the earth's resources.

For the Gaia Movement, the coming millennium is a crucial event that may spell the end of civilization or its rebirth, "a razor's edge in time where we either rise above the past or become victims of it." Perhaps global warming will destroy us, or perhaps we will collide with an asteroid, or perhaps a great earthquake will occur. Accordingly, the movement is calling for humanity to join together in meditation at the same moment on January 1, 2000, to effect a positive change in the course of history. Gaians call this positive change the LightShift. On January 1, 2000, the LightShift will begin when people all over the world engage in a "silent meditation on the pure light within" from 12:12 A.M. until 1 A.M. Gaians believe that "this unified circuit has the potential of shifting the collective consciousness to a higher octave and transforming the course of history in a more positive direction." In other words, if everyone meditates, the combined power of everyone's meditation can change the world. The unified thoughts of so many people will create "massive waves of love and compassion—raising the consciousness of all humanity, to usher in this new millennium in the sweetest and brightest light." If the Gaians can make their vision come true, theirs is probably the most positive vision of all of the prophecies for the year 2000.

Finally, though, it is important to remember that prophecies about what will happen in the future often have been wrong. For example, the famous British science fiction writer H. G. Wells once prophesied what life would be like after World War II. He saw a time that would be full of total chaos similar to the Dark Ages, when a few weak governments would rule over crumbling and disorganized societies. He predicted that "there will be a return to primitive homemade weapons, nonmechanical transport, a new age, if not of innocence, yet of illiteracy." Obviously, he was wrong. As Dr. Billy Graham reminds us in *Approaching Hoofbeats*, only God knows when the end of time will come.

[illegible] from machines, the combined power of economics and meditation can change the world. The unified [illegible] will create massive waves of focused consciousness, raising the consciousness of all [illegible] of sweeping and positive [illegible] can make their vision [illegible] of all of the prophecies for the year 2000?

[illegible] important to remember that [illegible] will happen in the future often [illegible] the previous century [illegible] and what life would be like [illegible] that would be [illegible] similar to the Dark Ages [illegible] government would [illegible] predicted that there will be a return to [illegible] not [illegible] don't know when the end of the millennium [illegible]

Chapter 4

What Is Predicted?

Will World War III begin in the year 2000?

Many of the prophecies and predictions surrounding the year 2000 involve a World War III scenario. But what is the possibility that such a war could actually occur within the next few years? Many experts believe that since the fall of Communism in the early 1990s, the probability of a world war has decreased significantly. Throughout the Cold War period, people's greatest fears revolved around the idea that a conflict between the United States and the Soviet Union would escalate into a war involving all of the major nations of the world. Now that the Cold War has ended, isn't such a scenario unlikely?

Maybe, but then again, maybe not. Recently, Ken Alibek, a defector from the former Soviet biological weapons program, revealed that from 1975 to 1991, when the Soviet Union fell, Moscow had indeed been planning for World War III. The Soviets were preparing hundreds of tons of anthrax bacteria and many tons of smallpox and plague viruses, to be mounted and released on ballistic missile warheads in case a war with the United States began. Alibek claims that the bacteria and viruses could have been mounted for an attack on a few days' notice in the early 1980s. The last president of the Soviet Union, Mikhail Gorbachev, officially canceled this biological weapons program in 1990; the program was officially canceled yet again by Russia's President Boris Yeltsin in 1992.

However, Alibek says that the biological weapons program in Russia actually is still in operation under the name of "defensive research." Many experts in the United States believe that some of the program still exists, but they do not know whether it includes the development of offensive weapons. If this is so, perhaps there is the chance that our fears of a third world war may be justified. The question is whether and why Russia would want to launch such an attack at a time when it is a country so politically and economically weak and when it is spending most of its energy trying to recover from the fall of Communism. But as we will see in this chapter, there are other countries that may actually pose a greater threat of starting World War III than Russia.

Is nuclear holocaust a possibility in the new millennium?

As we saw in chapter 3, many prophets and religious leaders—including Dr. Billy Graham—have predicted that a nuclear holocaust will be the ultimate means of destruction that will bring on the Final Judgment. Some Christian prophets are convinced that such a holocaust is predicted for the millennium in Revelation, the final book of the New Testament. For example, Dr. David Reagan, an Evangelical minister, refers to Revelation 6:8, which says that a series of God's judgments will result in the death of one-fourth of mankind. Dr. Reagan points out that only nuclear weapons could cause such a huge number of deaths at one time. He believes that the prophecies in Revelation "have clearly depended upon a major technological breakthrough for their understanding" and that "we are living in the time of that breakthrough."

The fear of nuclear holocaust is not restricted to religious prophecies, however. In the Hollywood movie *The Peacemaker*, terrorists bribe senior Russian defense officials and hijack nuclear material from a Russian military train. The terrorists—who are victims of the war in Bosnia—make a portable nuclear bomb, which they plan to explode at the United Nations building in New York City. Unfortunately, many weapons experts say that this scenario is a real possibility. A former Russian secretary general, Aleksandr Lebed, recently revealed that 82 of the 132 portable—or "backpack"—nuclear bombs produced by the Soviet Union during the Cold War are missing. If these bombs were to fall into the hands of terrorists, they might easily be used to destroy hundreds of thousands of lives.

This news comes at a time when many people believe that with the end of the Cold War and the collapse of the Soviet Union, the nuclear threat has practically disappeared. For example, a top security bomb shelter that was built in the 1960s for government officials was recently turned into a storage facility to preserve old movies that belong to the Library of Congress. This seems to suggest that the government, at least, is no longer worried about nuclear war.

But there are other threats to national security besides nuclear holocaust. For example, biological weapons may actually be more of a danger now than nuclear weapons. The current concern over Iraq's store of biological weapons is one indication of this. In fact, the United States Air Force recently released a report that was designed to assess threats that the world may face in the next millennium. One scenario the Air Force imagined for a possible future was entitled "Gulliver's Travails." In it, foreign terrorists kill 250,000 people in 2002 with a biological weapons attack at the Winter Olympics in Salt Lake City. Could it be that even the U.S. military predicts the end of the world in the next millennium?

Could an environmental disaster destroy the earth?

The threat of a global disaster in the near future through environmental causes is a possibility that concerns both prophets and scientists. Where might an environmental disaster strike? There are several areas that may cause major problems in the next millennium.

The Millennium Institute, which keeps track of worldwide environmental conditions, has a list of "State of Our World Indicators" for dangerous environmental situations. Here are key areas of concern they list as "red alert" situations, as of 1998:

* In seven years, there will be insufficient farmable land in the Northern Hemisphere.
* In thirty-eight years, there will be insufficient farmable land in the Southern Hemisphere.
* In eight years, one-third of the world's species will become extinct.

* In twenty-two years, 80 percent of the world's crude oil supply will disappear.
* In fifty-nine years, the amount of carbon dioxide in the air will double.
* Every day, 104 living species become extinct.

In addition, the institute estimates that water availability for the world's population is currently approaching a dangerously low "yellow alert" level.

If this list is accurate, a combination of any or all of these elements could create a global disaster, with shortages of oxygen, food, fuel, and water causing widespread death and disease. Is this a realistic scenario? Scientists and environmentalists are constantly debating whether the world is really in such bad shape. Whether these predictions are right or wrong, many people are concerned about how long natural resources will last into the next millennium.

Is global warming the next big threat?

Many scientists believe that the high amount of carbon dioxide being released into the atmosphere is causing the earth's temperature to rise to dangerous levels. Greenhouse gases from the burning of fossil fuels emit this carbon dioxide into the air. As we saw in the section above, carbon dioxide levels are predicted to double within the next fifty-nine years. How might this trend affect the earth in the next millennium?

Top scientists, using advanced computer programs, have projected a scenario for the year 2100 that demonstrates what might happen if the temperature of the earth continues to rise. Freshwater from melting arctic ice could pour into the North Atlantic, shutting down part of the earth's huge system of undersea currents. As a result, the gulf stream, which warms winter temperatures in Europe, would be diverted. Within a few years, Europe would go into a deep freeze. Dublin, Ireland, for example, would take on the climate of a city in the Arctic Circle. Eventually, the European continent would go into a total deep freeze, like that of the Ice Age. Meanwhile, North America and other parts of the world would grow unbearably hotter.

Some scientists say that the odds of this happening are one in ten, if carbon dioxide levels double. However, other scientists say that there is no way to predict changes in the temperature of the earth or the effect they will have and that warming isn't necessarily bad. Some even say that higher levels of carbon dioxide will benefit many plants, which use the gas as part of the process of photosynthesis.

What new diseases and plagues could sweep the world?

In the past twenty years, more than thirty new viruses have appeared around the world. They include the infamous Ebola virus, which broke out in Africa and which causes its victims to slowly bleed to death. Unfortunately, it is likely that the number of such viruses will increase even more in the next millennium, bringing a host of new diseases into the world.

To add to the problem of multiplying new diseases, old diseases such as tuberculosis, malaria, yellow fever, and cholera are beginning to make comebacks. New strains of drug-resistant tuberculosis, for example, have spread from thirteen to forty-two states in the past six years alone. In countries all over the world, 10 percent of all new tuberculosis cases reported each year cannot be treated. Health experts say that as this resistant virus spreads, the next millennium may bring a worldwide epidemic of incurable TB.

According to C. J. Peters, chief of special pathogens at the Centers for Disease Control and Prevention in Atlanta, the problem is that viruses today are changing themselves faster than the rate at which humans develop immunity. These bugs also can adapt to changing environmental conditions and the latest vaccine in very little time and can thrive even in places such as molten rock, the bottom of the sea, and strong acid solutions. Viruses that have not yet adapted to living in humans may move from other plant and animal species to humans who lack immunity, such as children and people moving from the country to the city, where there are more unsanitary conditions. This spread of viruses among city dwellers, in turn, can cause the viruses to spread rapidly around the world, as so many people travel every day on airplanes.

The rapid overpopulation of major cities around the world also increases the likelihood that new plagues and diseases will break out in the coming years. These "mystery" viruses will multiply as more mothers work and life expectancy increases and as overcrowding in day-care centers and nursing homes create more germ-friendly environments. Finally, there is always the danger that these diseases could become weapons for terrorists, who can poison water supplies or infest air-conditioning systems with the germs.

What can prevent these dangerous bugs from spelling disaster in the next millennium? Adequate research funding, says C. J. Peters, is necessary so that researchers can study how viruses operate. Detailed plans for developing countermeasures against each new viral family must be made. So far, the funds for this kind of medical research are very scarce. And as managed care becomes more common in the United States, doctors are becoming more reluctant to order expensive laboratory tests that could contribute to the early detection and control of new viruses, which furthers the danger that plague-like conditions could rapidly arise.

Is the population about to explode?

According to the Millennium Institute, the rate at which the world population increased in 1995 was 215,847 people per day. Three years later, that rate is 217,467 people per day. This is a "red alert" number. The current world population is 5,901,285,756. Twelve billion people is the maximum population that some experts think the earth can sustain. Others believe that the number of people the earth can support at a decent standard of living is only 1.5 to 2 billion, which we've already surpassed.

How long will it take for the population to reach 12 billion? If birth and death rates remain the same as they were in 1990, we will reach that number in 2028. At the very least, some experts say, the number will be 8.35 billion. However, the U.S. Census Bureau predicts a world population of only 9.4 billion by 2050.

What are the consequences of this rapid population increase? One expert on food policy, Per Pinstrup-Anderson, has said that "failure to significantly reduce the current high population growth rates in Africa within the next ten to twenty years will render all other development efforts insufficient to avoid future famines, degradation of land and forest resources, poverty, and human misery of much greater magnitudes than experienced to date." According to other experts, this kind of scenario will occur all over the world in overpopulated areas if population growth is not reduced. And, as we have seen above, overpopulation also increases the chance that viruses will spread deadly diseases throughout the world.

Will UFOs invade us?

Some people believe they already have. Somewhere in the Nevada desert, there is a secret government air base known as Area 51. Built in the early 1950s, Area 51 is patrolled by camouflaged security guards. To this day, the Pentagon refuses to confirm or deny that it exists. Many people believe it is the site where the government holds captured UFOs for study, and there have been reports of mysterious lights in the sky above the base. The Hollywood movie *Independence Day*, in which aliens attack the earth, contains scenes of an alien life form being held in captivity at Area 51.

Today, many people who believe in UFOs come to Area 51 to share their stories. For example, an engineer named Bill Uhouse claims he worked with an alien named Jarod to create a flight simulator based on extraterrestrial technology. And Bob Lazar claims that he saw several flying saucers while working at Area 51. He says he was shown documents revealing that in "the course of modern human history, three spiritual leaders, including Jesus Christ, had been artificially created by alien engineers." Many others have similar stories of alien contact or of sightings of UFOs.

As the millennium approaches, fears or hopes of an alien invasion have increased. In chapter 2, you read about the cult group in Garland, Texas, that believes aliens will come and save it from nuclear holocaust before the millennium. Even some respected experts seem to believe in aliens.

David M. Jacobs, professor of history and ufology (the study of UFOs) at Temple University in Philadelphia, has written a book called *Threat: The Secret Alien Agenda*. In this book, Jacobs states his belief that a race of alien pod-people is about to take over the world. For decades, he claims, aliens have been carrying out abductions of humans in order to crossbreed them with their own kind. Soon, the crossbred beings will join with the aliens in an invasion of the earth.

Jacobs says it may already be too late to stop the threat of "alien integration." He says that the aliens could land as soon as 1999. But although his book contains interviews with many people who claim they have been abducted by these aliens, no photographs, videotapes, or actual evidence exists to back up their claims.

The stories of those who claim to have had contact with aliens may sound far-fetched, but even the National Aeronautics and Space Administration (NASA) is putting more time and money into searching for life on other planets. The agency is beginning to fund the new scientific field of astrobiology, which seeks to find out what life in other worlds might look like and how it might have begun. Their new Astrobiology Institute is aimed at answering the question "Are we alone in the universe?" NASA also is in the second year of a program called Origins, which is partly devoted to discovering life on Mars and other places in space, such as beneath the crust of Jupiter's moon Europa. And a privately funded NASA program called the Search for Extraterrestrial Intelligence is looking for more advanced alien life through radio signals picked up in outer space. So far, none of these programs has found anything resembling advanced life forms.

Will an asteroid destroy the earth?

An invasion of aliens is not the only thing from outer space we could choose to worry about. On March 11, 1998, an astronomer named Brian Marsden announced that a mile-wide asteroid named XF11 was heading for earth and could crash into it on October 26, 2028. The announcement immediately set off widespread panic. But the next day it was announced that, in fact, XF11 would miss the earth by 600,000 miles.

Still, the realization that an asteroid could come so close to the earth within thirty years caused many people to think about the potential dangers we face from outer space in the next millennium. For example, some astronomers predict that deadly clouds of interstellar gas are coming our way. Some also believe that another galaxy is on a collision course with ours and that the sun could swell one day to the size of the earth's orbit, burning up our planet.

Of course, the odds of these things happening within the next thousand years are not very great. Asteroids remain an unknown but potential danger in the future. Ninety percent are still undetected and uncharted, and conceivably any one could hit us at any time. Yet statistics experts place the odds of being killed by an asteroid at 1 in 20,000, the same as dying in a plane crash.

What would happen if an asteroid hit? Even an asteroid only six-tenths of a mile wide would hit the earth with a blast equal to exploding all of the planet's nuclear weapons at once. An impact like this happens about once every 500,000 years. It is thought that dinosaurs were wiped out 65 million years ago by an object more than six miles in diameter. But even an asteroid less than a mile wide would cause global damage. Clouds of debris thrown into the atmosphere would darken the world for weeks or months. Huge earthquakes would rock the continents, and temperatures would plunge. Fires would spread out of control, and the food chain would collapse.

Just like in the movie *Asteroid*, scientists believe only a nuclear missile launched from the earth might obstruct an approaching asteroid's path. Unfortunately, this would be possible only if the asteroid were discovered several years before it was scheduled to hit. And with present technology, it would take at least a decade to find all of the 2,100 large asteroids that cross the earth's orbit. Since the scare over XF11, NASA has more than doubled the annual funding for research into tracking asteroids.

Can the economy endure?

In the late 1990s, America is experiencing an economic boom unmatched in its history. But can the boom last? And will the stock market continue to climb at unheard of rates?

Economists, who very seldom agree on anything, are divided about what the future will bring. Some say that the boom will continue, while others say that an event similar to the near-collapse of Japan's economy is destined to occur in our country in the next millennium—maybe within the next ten years. In fact, the collapse of the economies of several Asian nations has already had a bad effect on the U.S. economy. If countries such as Japan cannot afford to buy American products, our economy will suffer, too.

The New Age prophet, The Lord Maitreya, whom we met in the last chapter, has predicted that the stock market will crash in the year 2000 because of the energies that will be released by the constellation of Aquarius. This economic collapse, The Lord Maitreya claims, will begin with the fall of the Tokyo stock market and is necessary for humanity to redeem itself by redistributing the world's wealth.

However, the greatest threat to the economy for the millennium will probably not be the energies emitted by a constellation in the sky. In fact, it may be the problem we will discuss in chapter 9: the year 2000 computer bug, also known as the Y2K problem. Many, if not most, of the world's computers are not programmed to register the year

2000 in their memory banks. If they are not reprogrammed, the computers will crash, and a major economic crisis could result. For example, systems failures could cost the global foreign exchange market billions of dollars in a single week, causing major disruption in the world's financial markets. Even a single system failure could cause a domino effect in the global marketplace. The trouble is, it is very unlikely that every individual business and banking institution will have reprogrammed their computers in time for the year 2000. Therefore, the economy may be in grave danger sooner than we think.

However, some experts are optimistic that the next millennium will bring more prosperity to the United States. For example, in *Prosperity: The Coming Twenty Year Boom and What It Means to You*, Bob Davis and David Wessel predict that the globalization of our economy, the coming boom in new computer jobs, and the increased opportunities for job training in community colleges will bring increased prosperity to America.

What will happen to Social Security?

Will the Social Security system last into the next millennium? There is serious doubt that it will unless changes are made to the system. The problem is that the 76 million baby boomers will all reach retirement age in roughly the same period of time. By the year 2029, when all people born between 1945 and 1964 will have turned sixty-five, Social Security will have only enough money to pay 75 percent of the promised benefits to these people. This problem will be made worse by the fact that large numbers of baby boomers are not saving enough money toward retirement. What can be done to prevent the system from collapsing and leaving millions of retirees without enough money to live on?

President Bill Clinton proclaimed 1998 as the year for debate and discussion about Social Security, with 1999 as the year for taking action in Congress. Some groups argue that the only way to save Social Security is through increased taxes, reduced benefits, or an increase in the retirement age. Others say that the government should allow people to divert some of their payroll taxes into private investments such as individual retirement accounts. This solution could be a problem if private investments do not pay at their promised rate of return. As it is, the government bears the risk of bad investments; a shift to private investment also would shift that risk to the individual.

In addition, Social Security pays for more than just retirement. It also pays disability benefits and benefits to the widows and children of deceased workers. If Social Security loses money to private investments, will there still be enough money in the system for these people? Either way, it seems certain that some kind of changes must be made to the system. Otherwise, the next millennium will find retirees coming up short financially.

Could computers take over?

Although computers will undoubtedly continue to bring many wonderful benefits to humankind in the next millennium, they may also pose some grave dangers to the safety and security of the world. Computers themselves are not the problem, but the way people use them could be.

One of the greatest threats to national security could be sophisticated computer hackers who could use computer viruses to bring down banks and stock exchanges and cripple vital government infrastructures. This type of threat is called cyberwar or I-War (for information war), and many experts and government officials believe it is very real. A Third World country or a small terrorist group could wage this kind of war on a superpower like America and win. In fact, the more a country relies on complicated technology, the more vulnerable it is to this kind of war. Since almost all of our transportation, banking, security, and information systems are computerized, we run the greatest risk of a total shutdown of our society if we tamper with these computers. And perhaps the enemy could well be an anonymous person with a laptop computer.

A recent article in *The Independent*, a London newspaper, discussed the kinds of scenarios Pentagon officials imagine if a cyberwar erupted. One dramatic scenario goes: Computer terrorists tap into computer systems all over the country and cause disaster in just three days. On Day One, the telecommunications system in Texas shuts down; the signals on the railway between Washington and New York City fail, causing a terrible head-on collision between trains; and the air traffic control systems at major U.S. airports collapse, setting off huge delays and cancellations everywhere. On Day Two, the power goes out in four northeastern states, Denver's water pumping stations are disabled, and the computer records of all patients at Chicago's largest hospital disappear. On Day Three, the power fails in major American cities, the traffic lights in Manhattan stop functioning, America's spy satellites over the Middle East go blind, and American officials in foreign countries are kidnapped.

Such a series of events would result in major chaos, and it could be initiated by someone with a very sophisticated knowledge of computer systems. Pentagon experts say that it may take ten to twenty years to create the kind of technology necessary to prevent this kind of computer espionage. Some military experts believe that the threat of computer viruses and other interference is more dangerous and deadly than any nuclear or biological weapons.

Another, perhaps even more bizarre, threat from computers sounds like a scenario from science fiction. What if in the future, humans could become infected by computer viruses? One Japanese scientist says that as we approach the time when people will control computers with their voices or eye movements, "it is only a small step from us controlling them to them controlling us." He adds that true artificial brains for computers will be built within fifteen years, possibly controlled by our nerve impulses—such as blinks of the eyes. He even suggests that a computer virus could travel backward over the nerve interface and infect the human host. "It would not have a serious effect," he claims, "but short-term memory loss or impaired motor functions are a possibility." Experiments have demonstrated that technology could cause ill effects in human users. For example, fax machines cause epileptic fits in small rodents. Yet it seems far-fetched that computers could cause real illnesses in the people who use them.

Perhaps we fear computer control because of their amazing capabilities. According to Moore's Law (developed by Gordon Moore, the codeveloper of Intel computer chips), computers double their intelligence every eighteen months. They are already 130,000 times smarter than when the first computer silicon chips were invented in 1971. Moore's Law will apply for at least another fifteen years, by which time computers will be one thousand times more powerful than they are today. Computer scientists predict that in the next millennium computers will be able to design themselves, with no help from us. They will use "thinking material" superior to ours with which they can make themselves even smarter. Deep Blue, the computer that beat Gary Kasparov, the world's greatest chess player, is only a hint at how smart computers will be in the future.

Scientists are searching for ways to increase the chances that future computers won't have the same destructive potential for evil that humans do. But this, of course, depends on how smart we humans become about their use.

How long before scientists discover cures for cancer and AIDS?

Unfortunately, it will probably be many years into the next millennium before a true cure for either of these deadly diseases is found. The problem is that understanding these diseases requires mastering whole areas of knowledge that scientists are only beginning to understand. For example, imagine how long it will take to understand the extremely complicated process by which healthy cells malfunction, divide, and turn themselves into cancerous tumors. The process involves the interactions of hundreds of thousands of proteins and genes in the human body. Many scientists spend their entire careers studying only one of these genes or proteins—and may never be able to figure out how that one gene or protein works.

However, great strides have been made in detecting and treating cancer and AIDS. Scientists can now identify some of the genes that cause cancer, and they're beginning to understand the process by which ordinary cells become cancerous. Genetic testing—which tests people's genes to see if their genetic makeup predisposes them to certain cancers—is a relatively new way of diagnosing potential cancers. It's a long way, however, from providing a cure. The most effective treatments for cancer remain chemotherapy and radiation, both of which, unfortunately, kill healthy cells as they kill cancerous ones.

In AIDS research, scientists are developing medicines that can keep people who are infected with HIV—the virus that causes AIDS—alive much longer than was possible even a few years ago. These drugs are adding years to the lives of many people who would have had shorter lifespans sixteen years ago, when the disease was first identified. But scientists don't expect a vaccine against the virus to be developed for another ten years. Meanwhile, an estimated 600,000 to 1 million Americans are currently living with HIV.

Although the spread of AIDS seems to be leveling off among Americans in general, it is increasing among teenagers. One in four new HIV infections occurs in a person under age twenty-two, according to the Centers for Disease Control and Prevention. This means that in the next millennium, a new epidemic of AIDS could spread among young people that would rival the one that occurred a decade ago.

Are human clones a possibility?

People have been discussing the possibility of cloning humans for many, many years. Woody Allen's comedy film *Sleepers*, which takes place in the futuristic world of 2073, contains a scene in which scientists attempt to clone a world leader who has recently died. When the movie came out in 1973, the idea of cloning humans seemed not only silly but also far-fetched. But just twenty-four years later, in 1997, scientists in Scotland cloned an entirely new, identical sheep from the cell of a live adult sheep. Dolly, as the world's first cloned mammal was named, has become the most famous sheep in the world—and also has made human cloning seem a much more real possibility than anyone ever imagined.

Already the debate is raging about whether humans should be cloned. An American biologist, Dr. Richard Seed, announced early in 1998 that he could create the world's first human clone within two months. But as soon as he made the announcement, President Clinton proposed a total ban on human cloning in the United States. Protests against human cloning from religious and world leaders quickly followed.

What are the objections to human cloning? Many people feel that engineering humans from genes is like playing God—that creating human life outside of natural procreation is wrong because only God has the power to create life. Others feel that the individuality of human beings would be destroyed if scientists could make replicas of us from our genetic material. Evil people might clone humans for their own purposes, perhaps creating a race of "super beings" that could destroy the human race. Or perhaps people would take the opportunity to create only a certain kind of person—parents would choose to create only children with "perfect" characteristics (for example, blond hair and blue eyes) and high intelligence.

Others contend that human cloning could have great benefits. Dr. Seed points to the large number of couples who cannot have children for whom cloning could provide offspring. The *New England Journal of Medicine* opposes the ban on human cloning in light of all of the positive discoveries that could come from researching human cells. For example, cloning experiments on human cells and tissues could provide valuable information about aging and the causes of cancer.

Despite the objections, some experts believe that cloning humans will happen someday. As Dr. Seed has said, "If not me then someone else, if not now then later, if not in the United States then somewhere else."

What are some of the new inventions expected in the next millennium?

Designers and futurologists—people who study future trends—are already busy thinking up and creating models of products and services for the next millennium. What do these students of the future predict? Wristwatch phones may be the next big thing in the year 2000. ATMs will be able to identify customers instantly by electronic "eyes" instead of personal identification numbers. Cameras will be equipped with film that allows photographers to caption a picture as soon as it's taken. When the picture is processed, the caption will be automatically included in the frame.

In the home, intelligent refrigerators that are run by magnets and that automatically regulate food temperatures, self-cleaning bathrooms, and bathroom mirrors that offer a choice of TV and information channels while you brush your teeth will become common. Bedroom "hearts," which look like ordinary bedside tables, will control lighting and temperature and provide atmospheric sounds and images while you sleep. In fact, a software system for computers will allow people to run their entire homes through voice commands. Household appliances will be regulated simply by saying the words "on" and "off."

Children will be entertained by robotic pets and "ludic robots"—small, unpredictable electronic friends that respond to voice commands and touch. Parents will be able to keep tabs on their children with electronic tracking devices. Clothing will become more adaptable, offering bonus features such as built-in radios that can be switched on with the turn of a button or the zip of a zipper. Shoes will be made so that they can be cooled in the refrigerator on hot days and heated in the microwave on cold days. Some will come with inflatable soles to make them more comfortable. The first new man-made fiber in thirty years is being developed; it is made of wood pulp but feels like silk.

For leisure, people will be able to go to oxygen bars, where they can breathe pure air through tubes while listening to music and talking with friends. An item called a hot badge will come in handy for singles who want to meet new people at the oxygen bar. The badge stores information about the owner's interests, and when it comes into contact with another badge, it will send out a signal if the wearers' interests overlap.

In law enforcement, the National Institute of Justice is looking for new ways to stop gunmen without hurting innocent bystanders. Low-impact lasers could stop criminals by temporarily blinding or confusing them but would not cause permanent damage. Another harmless device would stop gunmen in their tracks by sending out low-frequency sounds that would make them nauseous. The National Institute of Justice also is working on "automating" police cars with document scanners, which would instantly transmit pictures of criminals or missing persons to police cars in every part of town.

A 1997 *Time* magazine article reported that in the next millennium, doctors will be able to "grow" body parts from cells to replace damaged ones. Houses and cars will be made of materials that can fix themselves when they are damaged. And a white, powdered food made of 90 percent protein will have the characteristic of being able to taste like any kind of food.

Futurologists also predict that as computers become cheaper, homes commonly will have more than one. The computers will instantly respond to voice commands and will respond in turn by speaking. The Internet will be a major source of shopping and entertainment, with the ability to broadcast movies, television-like programs, and live sporting events. Screens will be interactive, meaning that people will be able to talk to the people on the screen, interrupt the action, and change the camera angles. The Internet also will be an alternative means of transmitting faxes (they're usually transmitted over phone lines), which will dramatically cut the cost of worldwide communication. And as this kind of communication ability becomes more common, more and more people will work at home. In fact, some people believe that large corporations and organizations will break down into smaller parts as the Internet allows individuals to communicate directly with people all over the globe for very little money.

What will everyday life be like in the next millennium?

In her latest book, *Clicking: 17 Trends That Drive America*, Faith Popcorn—considered a reliable forecaster of everyday life in the future—has drawn a vivid picture of what ordinary life will be like in the next millennium. Popcorn is chair of BrainReserve, a marketing consulting firm that tells businesses which new trends will take hold in the future. Popcorn's previous book, *The Popcorn Report*, is often cited by businesses as perhaps the most accurate report ever published on consumer trends. So how, according to Popcorn, will the average American be living in the next century?

Popcorn envisions a future where more people will be spending their free time at home (or, as Popcorn calls it, cocooning) than ever before. This is because everything they need will be right there. People will plug into virtual reality machines, which will provide access to schools, games, books, movies, art, and just about every other kind of information and entertainment resource. At some point, microprocessing chips will be implanted in the human body, allowing anyone to store all kinds of knowledge in their brains, including the ability to speak other languages instantly.

Time away from home will be spent with organizations or clubs (Popcorn calls it clanning) or taking fantasy adventure trips to exotic travel destinations. Spiritual and family-oriented activities will become more and more important in our lives. For those who have what Popcorn calls millennial shakes, or fear of the year 2000, she has proposed an idea of her own: laser therapy that will allow people to erase painful emotions or memories. Antisocial behavior, she believes, also will be fixed this way. And for those who want to maintain a youthful appearance while they're cocooning? Do-it-yourself plastic surgery kits are on the way.

Will the United States be the leader among nations?

Although it seems unlikely that the United States will give up its role as the most powerful, influential nation in the world, some experts have painted a different picture of the country's future. One of the most pessimistic is Samuel P. Huntington, a political scientist from Harvard University. In his book *The Clash of Civilizations and the Remaking of World Order*, Huntington predicts that as the year 2000 approaches, the Islamic world will gain great power. He also predicts that China and Japan will join forces against the United States in a global conflict. Meanwhile, America will be led to the brink of civil war and will break apart because of warring immigrant and ethnic groups. Clearly,

Huntington does not believe that the United States will remain the leader among nations.

The Fourth Turning, a book by a pair of futurists named William Strauss and Neil Howe, portrays a similar fate for America. The authors predict that sometime during the first twenty years or so of the next millennium, a deadly civil war among the National Guard, urban gangs, and suburban militias may bring down the United States.

What is predicted for other parts of the world?

There are probably a hundred different predictions for every part of the globe, but a number of experts agree on a few things. Many scientists and political experts believe that the richest nations in the world—the United States and the countries of western Europe—will grow richer, while most poor Third World nations in Africa and Asia probably will grow poorer. Even those countries that have made economic gains in recent years could see their progress wiped out by disease or famine. For example, Botswana, a country that has one of the fastest growing economies in Africa, will undergo a severe crisis in the next millennium from an explosive rise in AIDS cases. Other growing countries, such as Thailand and India, are in similar situations, as the disease threatens to wipe out populations and large parts of the economy because of enormous medical expenses.

Another thing that is nearly certain is that conflict in the Middle East between Israel and the Arab countries will continue. Many people predict that terrorism by Islamic fundamentalists also will continue to grow. Saddam Hussein, the leader of Iraq, may continue to be a threat to world peace in the next millennium. The big question remains: Will war break out, triggering the global war that prophets like John Hagee have predicted?

Three important countries—Japan, Russia, and China—remain question marks, and their futures probably will have a major impact on the rest of the world. Will Japan recover from its recent economic slump? Will Russia dissolve into chaos or become a threatening world power again? Will China continue to open up to the West? Most important, will these countries be our friends or our enemies in the coming years? The answers to these questions will determine the fate of the world in the coming millennium.

Chapter 5

Is the Millennium Christian?

Is the millennium only a Christian event?

No. People all over the world will be celebrating the beginning of the third millennium, no matter what their religious beliefs. This is because the Gregorian calendar, which marks the millennium and which was originally a Christian calendar, is the most widely used measurement of time in most parts of the world. Even though other religions count time by different calendars, those calendars are usually used only to keep track of religious events. The Gregorian calendar, however, guides nearly all secular or nonreligious events around the world.

In fact, the year 2000 will mark the first time in history that there is worldwide recognition of a millennium passing. This event is unique, and Christians and non-Christian alike have cause to celebrate it.

However, the millennium has special significance for Christians because it marks the two thousandth anniversary of Christ's birth. In this sense, it is the occasion to reflect on the life of Jesus and on the important role of Christianity in the history of the past one thousand years. Also, some fundamentalist Christians believe that the millennium coming up will be the same millennium that is mentioned in Revelation, the final book of the New Testament in the Bible. In other words, it will be the end of time, or the beginning of Christ's thousand-year reign on earth.

But even this belief that the millennium will bring the end of the world and the dawn of a new heaven on earth is not restricted to Christians. Prophets of doom and disaster, religious and nonreligious, have foretold some kind of global catastrophe or ending in the year 2000, which will bring on the beginning of a transformed world. We have seen this belief in the prophecies of everyone from New Age seers to believers in UFOs to historians. The need to see the end of a period in time as the end of something else is universal. In fact, the term *millennium* has come to be used to describe any kind of ideal age or Golden Age after a catastrophic end.

For most mainstream Christian leaders and believers, the year 2000 will be a time of celebration and renewal, not a time of doom. And certainly, those who look at the calendar on the eve of the millennium—no matter what their religious persuasion—are likely to mark the passing of this extraordinary event in some way.

What is the relationship between Revelation and the millennium?

Revelation is the final, and some say the strangest, book in the entire Bible. It is the source of the belief of many fundamentalist Christians that the millennium is literally the time when the world as we know it will end and Christ's thousand-year reign on earth before the Final Judgment will begin.

Revelation is the only book of the New Testament that is classified as apocalyptic literature. Apocalyptic means a prophetic disclosure or foretelling of the future. Therefore, Revelation sometimes is known as the Apocalypse. Apocalyptic literature claims to give secret information about the coming times. It is usually full of symbols that only certain people can understand. It envisions a great Judgment Day when a messiah or deliverer will conquer evil and the righteous will be victorious. Apocalyptic literature usually promises that the time for this judgment is coming very soon. The Book of Daniel in the Old Testament, which we discussed in chapter 2, also is classified as apocalyptic literature. Other books of the Bible are historical accounts or lessons on the teachings of Christ. Revelation, however, is a vision of the End Time as revealed to Christ's disciple John.

The writer of Revelation describes himself as John of Patmos. He also is known as John the Divine and is thought not to be John the apostle. Patmos is a small island in the Aegean Sea. The evil Roman emperor Domitian apparently sent John to the island as a punishment for teaching the "word of God and the testimony of Jesus" (Revelation 1:9). Domitian, who reigned between the years 81 and 96 A.D., murdered thousands of Christians in his day.

Most Bible experts say that the writer of Revelation composed the book as a message to faithful Christians who were being brutally persecuted by Domitian and the Romans. Its vision of a final day of reckoning is a call to remain firm in faith and to remember that Christ will be victorious over the enemy in the end.

The second half of Revelation describes in vivid and confusing detail John's vision of God's Judgment. It is full of many strange symbols and visions that Christians in John's time would have understood but that we today have difficulty interpreting. Even Bible experts do not understand all of the sayings and prophecies contained in Revelation's second half. But through the ages, some Christians have interpreted the prophecies as applying to nearly any event to show that the end of the world is coming soon. Many of these prophets have focused on chapter 20 of Revelation, which describes John's vision that Satan is bound and thrown into a pit for a thousand years. During that time, martyrs are resurrected and reign with Christ. This thousand-year period of righteousness ends when Satan returns and is then defeated once and for all. The living and the dead are judged, and there is a new heaven and a new earth—the New Jerusalem.

Thus, some Christians believe that the upcoming millennium will be the millennial period described in Revelation 20. It will begin the thousand-year reign of Christ, to be preceded by a horrible world-ending battle with the forces of Satan. Some people believe this even though John warns at the beginning of Revelation that his words are intended only as symbols.

What events are described in Revelation?

The first three chapters of Revelation are mostly taken up with John's letters to seven churches in what is now

Turkey. The letters deal with problems in the churches and announce Christ's message: "He who has an ear, let him hear what the Spirit says to the churches" (Revelation 3:22). The most colorful events described by John in Revelation begin in chapter 4, when John is summoned through "an open door" in heaven and ascends to see the throne of God.

God holds a scroll sealed with seven seals. Only Christ is worthy of opening the seals. The opening of the seals reveals visions of the terrible wrath to be visited on the world. The Four Horsemen of the Apocalypse—conquest, war, famine, and death—are unleashed from the first four seals. The fifth seal is opened, and the cries of martyrs ring out. Then "the seal of the living God" reveals the salvation of the faithful, who number 144,000: "And they sing a new song before the throne and before the four living creatures and before the elders. No one could learn that song except the hundred and forty-four thousand who had been redeemed from the earth" (14:3). Many people have read this to literally mean that only 144,000 souls will be saved on Judgment Day. The seventh seal brings "silence in heaven for about half an hour."

A whole new series of visions begins with seven trumpets, heralding troubles even worse than those of the seals. Strange creatures appear, including a red dragon accompanied by "a beast rising out of the sea, with ten horns and seven heads" (13:1). This beast is generally interpreted to symbolize the evil Domitian and the Roman Empire. The creature harasses "a woman clothed with the sun" who gives birth to a child (12:1). She symbolizes the people of God, the Jews, and the church, pursued through the wilderness of the world. Another beast rises from the sea, bearing the number 666 (13:18). This number has become a widespread symbol for the Antichrist, although John probably meant it to represent another evil Roman emperor, Nero.

The seventh trumpet sounds and introduces seven bowls, which shower seven plagues upon the "great Babylon," a symbol of Rome and its wickedness. The sixth of these plagues prepares the way for the final conflict between God and the forces of Satan. The dragon and the beast gather "the kings of the whole world" for battle "at the place which is called in Hebrew Armageddon" (16:13–16).

What is Armageddon?

Armageddon is the scene of the final battle between the forces of evil—represented by the dragon, the beast, and the kings of the world—and the forces of Christ. The battle takes place in Revelation 16.16. *Armageddon* is a mysterious word that many Bible experts believe is a reference to Mount Megiddo, a place in Palestine that was the site of many Hebrew battles in biblical times. Revelation seems to imply that the "hill" on which the city fortress stood, or the mountain heights behind it, had also become a symbol of the final battlefield. For the Jews of John's time, it certainly was a symbol of the blood shed in defense of their religious beliefs. Other Bible experts believe Armageddon is the city of Jerusalem. Today, the word *Armageddon* refers to any kind of decisive or final battle.

Does Revelation discuss the Second Coming?

Yes, although John does not refer to this event specifically as the Second Coming. Before the final battle, Christ appears as the final horseman to lead the faithful into battle against Satan and his armies. The Christ described by John, according to his vision, is a king riding on a white horse. He has eyes like a flame of fire and a mouth like a sharp sword "with which to smite the nations" (Revelation 19:15). The cry of the martyrs that had been heard upon the opening of the fifth seal is finally answered. Satan is bound, and the resurrected martyrs reign with Christ for a thousand years.

The great white throne of God appears to John, and all of the dead are judged before the throne "by what was written in the books, by what they had done." The names of the faithful are recorded in the "book of life," and the damned are condemned to a "lake of fire and brimstone where the beast and the false prophet were, and they will be tormented day and night for ever and ever" (20:10). The damned will include "the cowardly, the faithless, the polluted, as for murderers, fornicators, sorcerers, idolaters, and all liars" (21:8).

What is the Messianic Age?

The Messianic Age describes the time when Christ will return to reign over the new heaven and the new earth. In Revelation, this time is described with great beauty and a sense of overwhelming happiness. A merciful God is with his people to "wipe away every tear from their eyes, and death shall be no more, neither shall there be mourning nor crying nor pain anymore, for the former things have passed away" (Revelation 21:4). Paradise is a city of "pure gold, clear as glass," the church becomes the bride of Christ, and all is perfection and glory. The faithful are in a constant and pure state of communion with God.

The term *Messianic Age* often is used to describe any arrival or return of a messiah or savior. It is the time when a savior unites with the faithful in a vision of eternal perfection and peace.

What or who is a millenarian?

Anyone who believes in the millennium described in Revelation—the thousand-year period during which Christ is to rule on earth—can be described as a millenarian. The word also is used to describe anybody who has faith in a hoped-for period of joy, serenity, prosperity, and justice at some time in the future. In fact, millennial visions predate Christianity by hundreds of years, as we will see in the coming chapters. For example, the belief in a soon-to-be period of relief from suffering can be found in the ancient Jewish prophets such as Isaiah, Daniel, and Enoch. Millenarians, no matter what their faith, believe they will be among those chosen to share in the glorious vision of the coming Golden Age. Millennial belief tends to rise during times of great social change or crisis. When times are bad, more people begin to long for a time of release from suffering.

In Christianity, as we will see, there are different types of millenarians, depending on how they envision the thousand-year period and when they believe it will arrive.

What are premillennialism and postmillennialism?

Almost since the beginning of Christianity, millennial belief has been divided into two categories. Those Christians who believe that the thousand-year period of righteousness in the world cannot begin until Christ comes to fight the final Battle of Armageddon are called premillennialists. Premillennialists take the vision in Revelation literally: At some point in history, things on earth will become so bad that the world will end in a horrible catastrophe. Christ must arrive with a heavenly host to vanquish the Antichrist at Armageddon. The faithful will be saved from this terrible battle and will reign with Christ for one thousand years in a paradise on earth. After this period, the Antichrist will be briefly unleashed again and finally conquered. The living and the dead will be judged in the Final Judgment.

Premillennialists live in the expectation that the end of the world will be sudden and terrible and may come at any time. They prepare for the end, believing that it will come in their lifetimes. Premillennialists throughout history have chosen various dates for the end of the world; as the time on the calendar closes in on the third millennium, some contemporary premillennial groups have fixed on the year 2000 as the End Time. Premillennialists are sometimes called apocalyptic because they believe that to achieve the millennium or Golden Age, a sudden revelation followed by catastrophe must occur. Apocalypse, you will recall, means a revelation of things that are hidden. Revelation is often referred to as the Apocalypse.

Postmillennialists, on the other hand, envision the return of Christ after the millennial kingdom has been perfected here on earth by human effort. Gradually, the Christianization of the world is taking place, and the millennial kingdom will be fulfilled without catastrophe by means of human cooperation with divine guidance. To postmillennialists, the task is to better the world in preparation for Christ's reappearance. In effect, the millennial kingdom was already established here on earth when Christ was born. Since then, postmillennial Christians have focused on making the world a better place until the Second Coming, which will occur peacefully and during which everyone will be saved. Postmillennialists do not set a date for the Second Coming; it is a spiritual destiny to be increasingly realized through the progress of humanity.

Did Christians believe anything special about the millennium in the years right after the death of Jesus?

Yes. In a sense, we can describe the earliest followers of Christ as the first premillennialists. During Jesus' time, there was widespread belief among Jews and Romans alike that the end of the world was near. It is believed that the followers of Jesus, too, expected that the world would soon end. After the Crucifixion, these early Christians were severely persecuted for their beliefs; one thing that kept the faithful strong and hopeful was the idea that Christ's Second Coming would happen during their lifetimes. During the first hundred years of Christian history, this form of premillennialism was commonly taught and accepted within the church. And it was in this atmosphere of persecution that John of Patmos wrote Revelation, which promised these early sufferers that the immediate aid of God was to be expected at any minute.

As Christianity became more and more accepted and persecution ended, the church began to place more emphasis on salvation within the soul of the believer rather than on a specific time when God would save the world. Saint Augustine, who lived from 354 to 430 A.D., taught that it was wrong for Christians to try to guess when the end of the world would come because "it is not ours to know this." He warned against reading current events as a sign that Judgment Day is coming. Rather, no supernatural event would intervene in history. According to Saint Augustine, the battle between good and evil had already been fought, and God had triumphed in heaven, or the City of God. It was up to believers to uphold their faith in the City of God and to resist the temptations of evil in this world. Revelation was to be read symbolically only, for to Saint

Augustine the millennium had already begun. It was a spiritual state the church had entered into after Christ's Resurrection. Eventually, God would be triumphant over Satan in this world as well, but not any time soon. This, more or less, remains the official doctrine of the Catholic Church to this day. Thus, the church was transformed from a premillennial group to a postmillennial one.

Were there any Christian premillennial groups before the twentieth century?

Yes. There have been many, many premillennial groups since the beginning of Christianity. As we will see, some mainstream religions contain premillennial beliefs. And throughout the past two thousand years, smaller groups or cults of premillennial believers that are more extreme in their beliefs have surfaced. These groups often meet violent ends or break up after their predicted dates for the final Battle of Armageddon do not hold true. These groups have been around, as we will see in the next chapter, since the early Christian era. After dying down for nearly a thousand years, they flourished during the Middle Ages and have been surfacing ever since, whenever there are times of great religious or political change.

What do Protestants believe about the millennium?

There are so many different kinds of Protestants that it is impossible to assign one particular belief about the millennium to all of them. Protestants are any of the many Christian denominations that trace their beginnings to the time of the Reformation in the early 1500s. This was the time when the German monk Martin Luther (1483–1546) led a movement that broke away from the authority of the

Catholic Church. Since then, many different groups of Protestants have formed. For example, Lutherans (the original followers of Martin Luther), Anglicans, Episcopalians, Presbyterians, Methodists, Baptists, and Evangelicals are all different kinds of Protestants.

Martin Luther himself did not believe in taking Revelation literally. Today, many mainstream Protestant denominations—such as Episcopalians and Lutherans—take the same position. They believe that the important battles of the End Time have already occurred, mainly during the Reformation, when Martin Luther's teachings allowed ordinary people to have more access to the Bible. Today, these denominations see their task as bettering the world until Christ comes again.

On the other hand, many evangelical, born-again, and fundamentalist Protestants believe that the final earthly battle has not been fought yet and that Christ will return to fight the Antichrist in their lifetimes. Many of these Christians are believers in the "rapture," an event when true Christians will be swept up into heaven as the Battle of Armageddon begins, saving them from the worldwide holocaust. Some fundamentalist Christians have begun a program of worldwide preaching called AD2000, in order to fulfill the words of Matthew 24:14 in the Bible: "And this gospel of the kingdom will be preached throughout the whole world, as a testimony to all nations; and then the end will come." In other words, they are hoping to bring on the End Time by spreading the gospel "throughout the whole world."

The return of the land of Israel to the Jewish people and the invention of nuclear weapons also have increased the belief that the end of the world is coming soon. Many fundamentalist Christians believe that these two events were prophesied in the Bible as signs that the End Time is nearing. Most born-again Christians do not set a specific date for this event, although as the millennium approaches, premillennial belief has become more widespread.

For example, at least one Evangelical Protestant church in South Korea, the Yoido Full Gospel Church, maintains a belief that events leading up to the battle of the End Time will begin to accelerate around the year 2000. The church's leader, Dr. David Yonggi Cho, believes that the Antichrist is already among us and that the establishment of a European Union will signal the beginning of the end. Dr. Cho's interpretation of the coming events closely follows the visions of Revelation, where the faithful will enter the millennial kingdom after a terrible battle during which 300 million people will die. At the end of a thousand years, there will be a Final Judgment, when unbelievers will be cast into the lake of fire.

Do Catholics believe the end of the world is coming?

The Catholic Church does not officially acknowledge or approve prophecies of doom, nor does it approve of predictions of when the End Time will come. Since the early church and the teachings of Saint Augustine, the Catholic Church has upheld the idea that the time of Christ's reappearance in the world is in God's hands. The new catechism of the Catholic Church says only that before the Second Coming, "the Church must pass through a final trial that will shake the belief of many believers."

In his address to the church's faithful, *Tertio Millennio Adveniente*, about the coming of the third millennium, Pope John Paul II discusses "a new springtime of Christian life which will be revealed by the Great Jubilee, if Christians are docile to the action of the Holy Spirit." Perhaps Pope

John Paul does hope for the return of Christ in the next millennium. Yet it is clear only that his vision of the year 2000 is full of hope for a spiritual awakening of some kind.

Over the past two centuries, a number of people—many of them children—have had visions of the Virgin Mary that are thought to have significance for the millennium. In some, Mary offers prophecies of the future and warnings about the fate of humanity.

The most famous vision occurred in 1917, in the village of Fatima in Portugal. Three peasant children reportedly saw the Virgin, who revealed to them three secrets. The first secret described a horrifying vision of hell. The second forecast that Russia would one day be consecrated to the Virgin Mary. The third secret has never been disclosed but has been read by three popes, including Pope John Paul II. Some people believe that the contents of this secret reveal a global disaster to come. Others believe that Mary predicted a great "Era of Peace" and divine mercy about to arrive in the coming millennium.

In another vision of Mary that occurred in 1983, the Virgin is said to have revealed that God had permitted Satan to take over the world in the twentieth century. But once this century is over, Satan's rule will end.

Are Jehovah's Witnesses, Seventh-Day Adventists, and Mormons premillennialists?

Yes. Jehovah's Witnesses, Seventh-Day Adventists, and Mormons are all Christian religions that were founded on the idea that Christ's Second Coming and the end of the world are near at hand. However, in recent years all three groups have moved away from predicting when the End Time will come.

Jehovah's Witnesses. The Jehovah's Witnesses were founded in the 1870s by a Pennsylvania clothing salesman named Charles Taze Russell. According to Russell's unique reading of biblical prophecy, Christ would begin his "invisible return" in 1874 and the world would end with Christ's Second Coming in 1914. The faithful interpreted World War I as a major sign that Russell was right, but the world did not end. Russell then declared that Christ in the form of the Archangel Michael had defeated Satan and established his kingdom in the outer heavens. The millennial kingdom on earth would begin "before the generation who saw the events of 1914 passes away."

Russell died in 1916, and his successor, Joseph Rutherford, took over. Rutherford directed followers to shun higher education, to avoid saving money, and to spend their time doing missionary work from door to door. He declared that only 144,000 followers would be taken up to heaven when the end came—a pronouncement in accordance with number of people saved in Revelation. All other faithful Witnesses would inherit a human paradise on earth as servants of the heavenly court. Witnesses endured severe persecution during World War II because the church forbids followers from entering military service or pledging allegiance to the flag. They believe that government institutions are unknowingly under Satan's control and should not be honored.

Since 1914, Jehovah's Witnesses have predicted that the end of the world would occur on a specific date many times. As the time nears when all of the members of the generation alive in 1914 will have died, some Witnesses believe that the third millennium will bring the End Time. But in 1995, the official magazine of the Jehovah's Witnesses, *The Watchtower*, announced that the group would no longer make predictions about the end of the world. The year 1914 still marks the beginning of the last days, but no one knows exactly when the end will come. Today there are more than five million Jehovah's Witnesses worldwide.

Seventh-Day Adventists. The Seventh-Day Adventists began as an outgrowth of the nineteenth century's Millerite Movement, which we will discuss in the next chapter. In 1844, William Miller predicted that the Second Coming would occur on October 22 of that year. When that prophecy failed, one of Miller's followers received a vision that explained why Christ had not come: Jesus had just begun an Investigative Judgment of the dead in preparation for his return to judge the living.

This vision, in turn, became the founding belief of the Seventh-Day Adventists, who were led by a housewife named Ellen White. White advocated observing the Jewish Sabbath—Saturday—and believed strongly that the millennium was at hand ("advent" directly refers to the coming of Christ). The Second Coming would not take place in America because the country is in league with the Devil. White identified it with the two-horned beast in Revelation.

White published her visions of the End Time in 1888 in a book called *Great Controversy*. Satan, in league with the U.S. government and the Roman Catholic Church, would persecute loyal Adventists until they were saved by Christ. Today, many Adventists have backed away from some of White's apocalyptic teachings. However, the belief that the end can be expected at any time is still important to them. Unlike Jehovah's Witnesses, the Adventists have never declared a date for this event. In 1995, the Adventists formally distanced themselves from anybody who sets dates for the end of the world or the Second Coming and stressed that any attempt to assign the date for the year 2000 is "misguided."

Mormons. Joseph Smith founded the Mormon Church, also known as the Church of Jesus Christ of Latter-day Saints, in 1830. Believers view Smith as a prophet who received the word of the Lord, which he translated into the Book of Mormon. The Latter-day Saints regard the Book of Mormon as holy scripture, along with the Bible.

The Latter-day Saints take their name from a line in Revelation: "For thus shall my church be called in the last days, even the Church of Jesus Christ of Latter-day Saints." Mormons believe that their church is the kingdom of God on earth, a divinely established institution through which God accomplishes his purposes in regard to the salvation of his children. The term *Latter-day* refers to the fact that Mormons believe their church was founded in what will be the last era of human history prior to the Second Coming of Christ. Smith himself believed that if he lived until his eighty-fifth birthday in 1890, he would see the Second Coming. But Smith was killed by a mob in 1844. His successor, Brigham Young, led his people to Utah, where the Latter-day Saints maintain their headquarters today.

Although Mormons believe and hope that the Second Coming will occur in their lifetimes, they discourage any follower from predicting or setting a date for its arrival. Instead, they concentrate on spreading the word of their faith around the world and on restoring what they believe is the true church (which they regard as the church when Christ was alive) in this world.

What does the Bible say about the millennium?

Biblical reference to the thousand-year reign of Christ can be found only in chapter 20 of Revelation:

> Then I saw an angel coming down from heaven. . . . And he seized. . .Satan, and bound him for a thousand years, and threw him into the pit, and shut it and sealed it over him. . . . Also I saw the souls of those who had been beheaded for their testimony to Jesus. . . . They came to life and reigned with Christ a thousand years. . . . And when the thousand years are ended, Satan shall be loosed from his prison and will come out to deceive the nations which are at the four corners of the earth, that is, Gog and Magog, to gather them together to battle. . . . But fire came down from heaven and consumed them, and the devil who had deceived them was thrown into the lake of fire and brimstone. . . . And I saw the dead, great and small, standing before the throne, and books were opened. . . . And if anyone's name was not found written in the book of life, he was thrown into the lake of fire. (20:1–15)

No other book of the Bible mentions this thousand-year period we call the millennium. The author of Revelation, John of Patmos, does not give a specific time for when the millennium will arrive, except to say in the beginning of Revelation that the book is about things that "must soon take place" (1:1). Revelation ends with the promise of Christ: "Surely I am coming soon."

Chapter 6

Apocalyptic Cults of the Past Two Thousand Years: What Did They Believe?

Throughout the history of Christianity, small groups of people with extreme beliefs usually have based their faith on the fact that the world would end very soon, probably violently. Some of these groups actively worked toward bringing about the End Time. Today, we call these groups cults. The more famous of them—Jim Jones's People's Temple, the Branch Davidians, Heaven's Gate—have become frightening symbols of fanatical behavior in our time. But many such groups have existed since shortly after the beginnings of Christianity. Here are brief histories of some of them.

The Montanists

As we saw in the last chapter, the early Christians expected that Christ would return to save them from the persecution of the Romans. Revelation was written as a kind of message to those who were suffering persecution under the emperor Domitian. It presented a full vision of the expected battle and the final reward for those who held on to their faith.

But soon Christian missionaries began to convert large numbers of Roman citizens, and the faith became accepted throughout the empire. The church began to concentrate on achieving spiritual communion with God in this world rather than waiting for direct divine intervention. Into this more organized and stable world came Montanus, a wild-eyed, charismatic prophet who was obsessed with dividing the past and future into units of prophetic calculation. Historians do not know much about Montanus except that in 156 A.D., he declared himself the prophet of a third testament, a new age of the Holy Spirit. His movement was located in Phrygia, an ancient country of west-central Asia Minor that is now part of Turkey. Apparently, Montanus would go into frenzied and ecstatic trances, claiming divine inspiration. His main vision was that the New Jerusalem was about to come crashing down into Phrygia, precisely between two Phrygian villages. The arrival of this New Jerusalem would usher in a "third age" of God's spirit.

Montanus and his followers gathered from all around to await the big event, praying and fasting and generally hoping for martyrdom. But the advent of the New Jerusalem never happened. It is believed that when it failed to arrive, Montanus and his priestess Maximilla committed suicide. However, Montanism as a movement survived for several hundred years after its founder died. The fanatical nature of Montanism caused the church to declare such prophecies and behavior as heresy—outside the accepted teachings of the church. And ever since the Montanist Movement, the Roman Catholic Church has frowned on any groups that claim to prophesy the Second Coming.

The Apostolic Brethren

In his book *The End of Time: Faith and Fear in the Shadow of the Millennium*, religious expert Damian Thompson describes the Apostolic Brethren as "one of the first 'doomsday cults.' " The group was founded in 1260 in Italy, at a time when that land was troubled by plague, famine, and religious war. The Brethren were led by a monk named Fra Dolcino, the son of a priest from Parma. They began by preaching that the Church of Rome was no longer operating under the authority of God. Instead, the Brethren were now the supreme authorities. Accordingly, they believed that the pope and all of the clergy in Rome would soon be destroyed by the "Last Emperor" in a great battle. After that, the Age of the Spirit would begin.

Like many modern-day cults, when the great battle did not happen, the Apostolic Brethren simply moved up the date of its arrival. At first they waited until the end of the 1200s. Then they predicted that the end would come in 1305. In preparation, they moved to a mountain stronghold in the Alps in 1304. Here they lived a very simple life, waiting for the coming war and preaching against the Catholic Church to the local peasants. The 1305 deadline passed. Then, in 1307, the Apostolic Brethren—with the locals' support—engaged in an armed confrontation with the forces of the church at Monte Rebello. All of the Brethren were killed, and the movement of the Apostolic Brethren died with them.

The Taborites and Adamites

Thompson describes the Taborites and their offshoot cult, the Adamites, as the "first large-scale millenarian movement before the Reformation to create an apocalyptic community." Whole towns converted to the Taborite Movement, which centered in Bohemia (now a part of the Czech Republic in eastern Europe) in the early 1400s. Again, the leaders—a band of ex-priests—were revolting against the authority of the Catholic Church. They took over an old fortress and renamed it Tabor, after the mountain in Israel where the Transfiguration of Christ took place.

The Taborites believed that the Second Coming would arrive between February 10 and 14, 1420. Everyone but the Taborites and their followers would die a fiery death, like the inhabitants of Sodom in the Old Testament. Meanwhile, Christ would come down and live with the Taborites in the new millennium, which would be paradise on earth. Peasants in the surrounding area, eager to be saved from the fire, soon joined the movement. They sold their possessions and donated all of their money to the Taborite cause. Small towns around Tabor were turned into communes where, as Thompson says, "brotherly love was intended to replace the rule of law." All possessions were to be owned in common, and "whoever owns private property commits a mortal sin."

But the spirit of brotherly love did not last long. When Christ failed to appear in February 1420, the Taborites organized a military force and began waging war all over central Europe. They believed they were the "army sent by God into the whole world to execute all the plagues of the time of vengeance." Their particular targets were the rich and the clergy: "All lords, nobles, and knights shall be cut down and exterminated in the forests like outlaws." Unless and until all sinners in the world were exterminated, Christ would not come to Tabor. Meanwhile, back in the Tabor townships, another apocalyptic group sprang up that was even more radical than the Taborites—the Adamites.

The Adamites believed they were the Saints of the Last Days mentioned in Revelation. They even believed that they were superior to Christ because, after all, his Crucifixion had proved that he was only human. And because they also believed they were incapable of sin, they basically ran wild, committing every sin known to humanity. Expelled from the Taborite towns, the Adamites captured an island in a river, where they practiced free love and danced naked around campfires. At night, they would ride into the countryside and kill anyone they encountered, burning down whole towns and stealing whatever they could find. They were especially happy to slaughter priests. The Adamites believed they were immortal and that they would live forever as inhabitants of the earthly millennium.

The Taborites finally overran the Adamite island and killed all but one of their followers, whom they burned at the stake. In 1434, the Taborites met a similar fate when a Bohemian army slaughtered nearly all of them.

The Anabaptists of Munster

The episode of the Anabaptist movement in Munster, Germany, may be one of the bloodiest in the history of cults. The movement was established at the time of the great religious upheavals caused by the Reformation, when Martin Luther broke away from the authority of the Catholic Church. The Anabaptists rejected both the Catholic Church and the followers of Martin Luther. Some Anabaptists were peaceful and God-fearing. But others were convinced that the end of the world was coming and that only they would be saved from damnation.

The most radical Anabaptists moved to Munster in 1534. They drove Catholics and Lutherans out of town and took over, claiming that Munster would be the site of the New Jerusalem in the last days. People were rebaptized as Anabaptists, and a strange religious fervor took over. Soon the sight of townspeople writhing and screaming in the streets from their visions of the Apocalypse became common. The local Catholic bishop quickly organized a military force outside the walls of the town and laid siege to it—no food or supplies could get to the Anabaptists. Inside, the situation got worse.

Jan Matthys, the leader of the Anabaptists, began terrorizing his own people, banning all books but the Bible and condemning to torture anyone who disagreed with him. One day, he ventured beyond the walls of the town and was cut to pieces by the bishop's forces. But he was replaced by an even crazier and more brutal leader, Jan Bockelson, who began his rule by running naked through Munster in a state of ecstasy. Bockelson announced that polygamy (the practice of having more than one spouse) was God's word; people who disagreed with this pronouncement were executed.

Soon Bockelson began to refer to himself as the King and Messiah of the Last Days. He took many teenaged wives and lived in splendor, demanding that the townspeople give him all of their possessions, money, and food. Meanwhile, because of the siege by the bishop's forces, his followers were starving. Bockelson proclaimed that the Second Coming would not arrive until every religious and political leader in the world had been killed. He would send followers into the country, where they would evade the bishop's men and go on murderous raids, attacking and killing anyone of wealth or position. Apparently, Bockelson believed that the beheading of huge numbers of townspeople also was necessary to bring about the last days—he even performed the beheadings himself.

Meanwhile, the siege of Munster continued. No food or supplies could pass into the town, and the people began to starve. They ate any animal they could find—including rats. They grew so weak that in June 1535, a surprise attack by the bishop's military easily conquered Munster. The Anabaptist leaders were killed immediately, except for Bockelson, who was slowly and publicly tortured to death with hot irons. The radical Anabaptist movement had finally seen its last days.

The Fifth Monarchy

Is it possible that a millennial group could actually topple an entire government? It almost happened once, in seventeenth-century England. During the mid-1600s, civil war raged throughout the country. King Charles I was beheaded in 1649, and there was no royal head of the country until 1660. Many different types of Protestantism developed, including Puritanism, which preached of strict religious discipline and the sinfulness of luxury and earthly pleasures.

In the feverish atmosphere of the civil war, millennial groups began to sprout up like mushrooms. The Ranters, the Muggletonians, and the Quakers were just a few of the religious sects that organized themselves at that time. One extreme group of Puritans was the Fifth Monarchy, so called because they believed that the time of the "fifth monarchy"—in other words, the one that would succeed the Assyrian, Persian, Greek, and Roman monarchies of world history—was at hand. During the fifth monarchy, Christ would begin his reign on earth with his saints for one thousand years.

The Fifth Monarchists believed that England should prepare for King Jesus' return, when death and famine would be abolished and the righteous rewarded. Government institutions, such as the tithing system (similar to taxes) and the courts, should be abolished and replaced by systems based on biblical ideals. The Fifth Monarchists planned to take over the government to achieve their goal of bringing about the reign of Christ. In fact, their supporters almost succeeded in taking over the English Parliament in 1653. The leader of the English government at the time, Oliver Cromwell, withdrew his support for them at the last minute.

After it became clear that the Fifth Monarchists would fail in their attempt to take over the government, they continued to hold rallies that often turned violent. One of their followers led uprisings in London in 1657 and again in 1660. Calling out for "King Jesus," the Fifth Monarchists were confronted by a regiment of official guards and lost forty men in the process. Their leader was executed, but not before declaring himself the Christ. For a brief time, though, a millenarian cult almost succeeded in taking over one of the most powerful countries in the world at the time.

The Millerites

Nineteenth-century America was a hotbed of millennial activity in somewhat the same way that the last part of the twentieth century has proved to be. In the early 1800s, so many religious revivalists—with their big tent meetings, passionate preaching and shouting, and public expressions of faith—passed through upstate New York that it became known as the burned-over district, for the fire of revivalism itself.

Out of this atmosphere of feverish religious activity came William Miller, a New York farmer and former army officer who was convinced, based on his readings of the Book of Daniel and Revelation, that the Second Coming was at hand. In 1832, Miller published his findings and calculations about the End Time: The "time of the end" had begun in 1798, and Christ's Second Coming would definitely happen sometime between March 21, 1843, and March 21, 1844. At that time, the world would be engulfed by fire, and the righteous would be taken up to heaven. Miller's calculations were so carefully worked out and apparently so convincing that he began to attract a large group of followers—the Millerites claimed at least 100,000 followers at the peak of their popularity. A comet that appeared in November 1833 only heightened the Millerites' sense that the end was coming.

But March 21, 1844, came and went, and Christ did not appear. A number of Miller's followers left the movement; others decided to figure out what had gone wrong with the initial prophecy. One of these followers came up with a more precise date for the Second Coming: October 22, 1844. On that day, hundreds of Millerites gathered on hillsides and waited for the advent of Christ, when they would all be delivered up to heaven. The sun went down, and still they waited. And waited.

The night of October 22, 1844, has gone down in religious history as "the Great Disappointment." Damian Thompson says that because of this humiliating experience the Millerites were subjected to the jeers and ridicule of neighbors and strangers wherever they went. And although the disappointed followers of William Miller went on to found the Seventh-Day Adventists, never again would they dare to prophesy an exact date for the arrival of the Lord.

The Counsellor of Brazil

At the close of the nineteenth century, a group of Brazilian peasants fled from the coast, with its economic hardship, to the interior of the country. There they found a small village they named Canudos. Their leader was sixty-year-old Antonio Conselheiro ("The Counsellor"), who believed that the overthrow of the Portuguese and the establishment of a Brazilian republic were the work of the Antichrist. Surely the end of the world was at hand, perhaps to arrive at the turn of the new century in 1900.

The Counsellor prophesied that the final years of the old century would bring many strange events. These prophecies are reported in Mario Vargos Llosa's book *The War of the End of the World*. They are repeated in Thompson's *The End of Time*. In 1896:

> Flocks would flee inland from the sea coast and the sea would turn into the backlands and the backlands into the sea. In 1897 the desert would be covered with grass, shepherds and flocks would intermingle, and from that date on there would be but one single flock and a single shepherd. In 1898, hats would increase in size and heads grow smaller. In 1899 the rivers would turn red and a new planet would circle through space.

These strange events would end in 1900, when "the sources of light would be extinguished and stars would rain down." These nonsensical prophecies would gain the Counsellor a following of 20,000 peasants, all of whom came to Canudos to wait for the end.

Although Canudos was nothing more than a miserable shantytown and all of the townspeople were dirt poor, the Counsellor and his followers easily defeated a band of 500 federal soldiers who had been sent in to settle a local dispute. The Brazilian government was outraged. Next, they sent a force of 1,300 troops armed with artillery and led by a skilled officer. But the troops were unprepared for the rough, unfamiliar countryside and the scalding heat. The Canudos peasants killed nearly all of them, along with their commander.

Finally, the government decided not to take any chances. It sent in an army of 10,000 men, along with five top generals. The Counsellor and his followers fought ferociously, burning down the town in an attempt to destroy the enemy. But on October 5, 1897, the army overcame Canudos. Not a single follower of the Counsellor was found alive. Canudos had been burned to the ground, its collection of shacks and huts reduced to a mere pile of cinders. Indeed, for the Counsellor and his faithful, the end of the world had come—three years short of the appointed date of 1900.

The Ghost Dance Movement

In his book *Questioning the Millennium*, scientist Stephen Jay Gould tells the tragic story of the Native American Ghost Dancers of the late nineteenth century. During the late 1860s and early 1870s, a time when Native Americans were being conquered and contained by white settlers and the U.S. Cavalry, two Paiute Indians from Nevada—Tavibo and Wodziwob—taught an old Native American tradition called the Ghost Dance to the tribes of California and Oregon. The ritual died down after Wodziwob's death in 1872, but Tavibo's son, Wovoka, revived it. Wovoka had studied with Mormon missionaries and had been raised by white Christians. He combined the Ghost Dance with ideas about the millennium that he had learned from his Christian teachers. He began to preach that if the Indians would do the Ghost Dance, they would experience a millennial renewal. As Gould explains it, "The ghosts of ancestors would return to dwell with the living; the land would be restored to its original cover, richness, and fertility; the white man would disappear; and the buffalo would return."

The Ghost Dance ritual spread among Native Americans from Texas to Canada like wildfire. Tribes would abandon their daily routines and dance for days, chanting and singing. The Sioux tribe added a new part to the ritual: If they wore a particular kind of shirt during the dance, the white man's bullets could not kill them.

Dancers reported seeing visions, as they performed the ritual, of the Great Messiah, who promised that the white man could no longer hurt them. They would see their ancestors and dead relatives and a land restored to its former bounty, before the white man had come.

Unfortunately, the whites watching these frenzied scenes of dancing did not understand what was going on. They became alarmed and wrongly feared that the Indians' vision of the millennium included the massacre of all whites. A Chicago newspaper's headline for October 28, 1890, read: "To Wipe Out the Whites: What the Indians Expect of the Coming Messiah; Fears of an Outbreak; Old Sitting Bull Stirring Up the Excited Redskins." The U.S. Indian Police went to arrest Sitting Bull, the famous Sioux chief and supporter of the Ghost Dance ritual. A gun battle broke out, and Sitting Bull was killed, along with six policemen and seven of Sitting Bull's men.

Two months later, white fears over the Ghost Dance caused the government to round up the Lakota Sioux tribe for confinement on a reservation. During the march to the reservation, at Wounded Knee Creek in South Dakota, government soldiers fired into a group of Indians attempting to escape. The Sioux fought back. By the time the battle ended, thirty soldiers were dead, along with eighty-four Sioux men, and sixty-two of their women and children. As Gould puts it, "The ghost shirts had not worked." The Ghost Dance Movement was officially over.

The People's Temple at Jonestown

In 1978, Jonestown, Guyana, was the site of the worst cult-related murder and suicide in modern history. That was where the members of the People's Temple, led by the self-proclaimed Reverend Jim Jones, had gone to found their "ideal" community of racial and socialist harmony.

Jones was a manipulative and charismatic leader who declared himself to be the reincarnation of Jesus Christ. Only true followers of his revolution would be saved from the evil of the rest of the world. Jones prophesied that the United States was "the beast" of Revelation and would be destroyed. The righteous would escape and found a new nation. Accordingly, he moved his growing group of followers—nearly all Americans from various ethnic and racial backgrounds—from San Francisco to a remote jungle in Guyana in the early 1970s. He believed that the police and the media were persecuting him and that before American society destroyed itself with greed and racism, it would bring on Armageddon by trying to destroy Jonestown. Followers would have to be prepared to sacrifice themselves in such an event.

But Jonestown turned out to be no haven of peace and harmony. A Jesuit priest in Guyana became alarmed by Jones's leadership in 1974, when Jones borrowed the priest's church for a lecture on agriculture. Instead, Jones performed "healings" on his followers, exhibiting bloody animal parts that he claimed were cancers pulled from the bodies of the sick.

When the priest began to investigate the People's Temple further, he became even more alarmed. Members were being starved and forced to work endless hours in the broiling heat, tending fields. Jones beat and humiliated anyone who questioned him, even burying troublemakers alive in underground boxes. In the meantime, Jones sat on a throne as his followers knelt before him and called him Father.

Members who tried to escape Jonestown were confronted by armed guards at the entrances. Even if they did escape, dense jungle surrounded them; the nearest city, Georgetown, was 140 miles away. Besides, members had given up all of their money and their passports to Jones. They were more or less prisoners in the compound, cut off from family and friends, to whom they were forbidden to write about their situation.

But a California congressman, Leo Ryan, had gotten word about the terrible situation at Jonestown. In November 1978, he organized a trip to Guyana with reporters and some of the cult members' relatives to investigate Jim Jones's compound. Jones ordered the congressman not to come, but he did anyway. After Ryan and his party toured Jonestown, he invited any cult members who wanted to leave to join him. Twelve members departed, but Jones sent an armed party after them. As Ryan and the others arrived at their airstrip, Jones's armed men began shooting. Five of the visitors were killed, including Congressman Ryan. The others escaped by pretending to be dead or by running into the surrounding jungle.

Meanwhile, back at the compound, Jones told his followers that the congressman's visit signaled the beginning of an all-out assault on the cult. He claimed that CIA-led Guyanese soldiers were advancing toward Jonestown, planning to torture, castrate, and murder them. In effect,

Jones created his own Armageddon scenario, initiating the final battle that would lead to the promised land. The only way to salvation, Jones said, was mass suicide—a strategy that cult members had rehearsed many times at Jones's command. This time, however, the ritual was not merely a practice run. The 900 members, including Jones, drank cyanide-laced Kool-Aid from a huge vat. Those who refused to take the poison were shot and killed with guns and crossbows. The screams of the dying were captured on a tape recorder left running at the time of the suicide/murder.

Today, the jungle has overrun what is left of the Jonestown compound. But some Guyanese, including the priest who first discovered the horrible nature of the cult, would like it preserved. They believe that with the end of the millennium coming, many other Jonestown-type cults could arise, ending in the same kind of tragedy. The compound, they say, would provide a valuable warning to the world of the dangers of such cults. If their plans are approved, it may be possible soon to visit the site of this bone-chilling memorial to millennial cults.

The Branch Davidians

On April 19, 1993, a standoff lasting fifty-one days between FBI agents and the Texas religious cult known as the Branch Davidians ended in a fire that consumed the seventy-one Davidians inside their compound. Men, women, and children died, along with their thirty-four-year-old leader, David Koresh. How did the infamous tragedy at Waco happen? And what were the religious beliefs for which Koresh and his followers gave up their lives?

The saga of the Branch Davidians begins with Koresh, who started life as Vernon Howell in 1959. His mother was an unmarried high school dropout who married, divorced, and remarried while Howell was growing up. As a boy, Howell was tossed back and forth between two families, his mother's and his grandparents', in a succession of small Texas towns. Howell claimed that as a child he was mistreated by his grandfather and beaten by his stepfathers. As a teenager, he was thrown out of high school and spent most of his time playing guitar, gaining the attention and admiration of younger neighborhood teens. He was handsome and charismatic, and young people seemed to worship him.

The only constant in Howell's life was the Seventh-Day Adventist Church, to which both his mother and grandmother belonged. He knew the Bible by heart, and after a brief break with the church, he suddenly returned to a congregation in Tyler, Texas, in his early twenties. Howell became obsessed with biblical scripture and prophecy. At first, he only wanted to learn more about scripture. But soon he was challenging the authority of the church elders and taking over the Sabbath services. Church leaders were concerned about his hold over the children in the congregation and about his aggressive, intense sermons.

To make matters worse, Howell had become captivated by a series of Revelation seminars conducted by a local evangelist. The seminars featured a multimedia show with frightening images of Armageddon—earthquakes, pestilence, and religious persecutions. They were combined with a video of current events that predicted the coming biblical millennium. Howell became convinced that there was something missing in the presentation: the seventh seal of Revelation, which could only be opened by a new prophet. Soon, Howell determined that *he* was that prophet.

The Seventh-Day Adventists of Tyler, frightened by Howell's aggressive ways, asked him to leave. He went to Waco, Texas, where he joined a small band of ex-Adventists called the Branch Davidians. Howell seized leadership of the Davidians in a shoot-out with another member in 1987. Soon he began calling himself David Koresh, after two biblical kings. During the next five years, he turned the Davidians' compound, called Mount Carmel, into an armed fortress that he renamed Ranch Apocalypse. He began actively recruiting new members, who would turn over their income and savings to the cult. Koresh preached that he was a sinful incarnation of Jesus Christ, claiming for himself all the women of the compound.

Koresh's teachings were based on an interpretation of Revelation in which the U.S. government is the source of all evil. The government would bring all of its power to bear against the Lamb (Koresh) and his elect, so the Davidians had to amass weapons and prepare to fight the forces of the Antichrist. Unlike many other apocalyptic groups, Koresh did not preach that he and his followers would be delivered up to heaven before the final battle of Armageddon. Instead, they would have to fight the forces of evil to the death in order to bring on their salvation.

On February 28, 1993, after investigating the Davidians for months, the Bureau of Alcohol, Tobacco, and Firearms raided the compound with warrants for weapons violations. A gun battle began, during which four federal agents were killed. The raid only further convinced the Branch Davidians that Koresh's prophecies were coming true: This was the opening round of the final battle. FBI agents surrounded the compound and for fifty-one days attempted to negotiate with Koresh to surrender. Some religious experts who were called in to help the FBI took Koresh's belief that he was the Messiah seriously and tried using biblical arguments to persuade him to come out. But the FBI, alarmed by charges of child abuse within the compound, lost patience with him. On April 19, they sent in tanks armed with tear gas. A fire suddenly erupted within Ranch Apocalypse. The Branch Davidians inside all perished.

Did the FBI's gas somehow set off the final fire, or did Koresh himself ignite it to fulfill his prophecy? Most people believe the latter is true, but experts also maintain that the FBI's choice to launch the final assault assured the destruction of the Davidians. The government played the part of evil beast just as Koresh had prophesied. In order to carry through his vision, he and his followers had to die.

Was Waco a tragedy that could have been avoided? Nobody knows the answer for sure. But Michael Barkun, an authority on religion, has warned that there will be more Wacos if law enforcement officials "naively become coparticipants in millenarians' End Time scripts."

Aum Shinrikyo

The Aum Shinrikyo cult from Japan is one of the most sinister and dangerous millennial cults of all time. Apparently, the leader of the group was prepared to start the final Battle of Armageddon by mass-murdering hundreds of thousands of Japanese with sarin. Sarin is a lethal nerve gas many times more poisonous than cyanide.

On March 20, 1995, cult members released sarin into the crowded Tokyo subway system, leaving twelve people dead and 6,000 injured. It was not the first time the group had used sarin to commit murder, nor, apparently, was it the last attack the group had planned. An earlier sarin attack in the Japanese town of Matsumoto had left seven people dead and two hundred injured. It is believed that Aum was trying to produce seventy tons of sarin, which it planned to spray from helicopters all over Tokyo and other Japanese cities. A plan to secure nuclear weapons was also in the works. The cult had only 10,000 members in Japan, but it had the potential to cause destruction on a scale unimagined by any previous millennial group. How did it happen?

Shoko Asahara, the leader of Aum Shinrikyo, was born in 1955 as Chizuo Matsumoto. Early on, this half-blind son of a weaver developed an interest in mysticism. His transformation into a prophet occurred when he suffered great humiliation: He failed his entrance exams to Tokyo University. Shortly afterward, he began to have visions that he was a messiah. In the 1980s, at a time when Japan was achieving great prosperity, Asahara was preaching that salvation could be achieved only by giving up material success and by undergoing great suffering. Accordingly, many of the cult's members were young, middle-class professionals who felt their successful lives had not brought happiness.

Aum Shinrikyo members gave up everything and were subjected to sleep and light deprivation rituals—common brainwashing techniques. Many of them were told to give up their homes and families and to live in special Aum communes. Members who rebelled were injected with dangerous drugs or even lynched. Murdered cult members were often incinerated in specially built microwave ovens.

At first, Asahara taught that evil energy spreading throughout the world would bring about mass destruction in 1999. To avoid this event, 30,000 believers would be needed to convert the evil energy into positive energy. This could be done only by following Asahara. Later on, his message changed. Armageddon could not be prevented, but Asahara's followers could survive and build a new world if they practiced special breathing exercises. These exercises would allow them to survive the chemical, atomic, and biological weapons used in the great battle.

Asahara's prophecies combined elements of ideas from Hinduism, Buddhism, Revelation, and even the prophecies of Nostradamus.

By 1993, Asahara's followers were living with a constant sense that the end was near. The core members of the group moved to the base of Mount Fuji, Japan's highest mountain, where they set up a commune complete with divisions for chemical and gas manufacturing. Somehow Asahara's prediction of a coming doomsday had turned into a need to bring on that doomsday himself, and his followers began producing deadly chemicals under his command. Death, Asahara preached, would bring about spiritual awakening for both the murderers and their victims. No one knows exactly when Asahara decided to turn his prophecy of Armageddon into a reality, but when the gas attack in the Tokyo subways occurred, Japan finally realized the deadliness of this cult.

Asahara is currently behind bars in Japan, where he and many of his followers are on trial for murder. The frightening thing is, Asahara is still worshiped by thousands of believers in his prophecies. It is thought that at least 5,500 Japanese still follow his teachings, and these followers are recruiting new members to Aum Shinrikyo every day. They believe that Asahara was unfairly targeted by a government conspiracy, even though numerous former Aum members have testified that Asahara ordered a number of murders, including the subway gas attack.

Heaven's Gate

On March 26, 1997, police broke into a luxurious home in a wealthy San Diego neighborhood on a tip that something was wrong inside. What the police found in the spacious villa shocked and puzzled them. Eighteen men and twenty-one women were laid out on bunk beds and covered with purple cloths. Each body had an identification tag attached to it, and some of their heads were covered with plastic bags. It turned out that those inside this compound had committed suicide by eating applesauce laced with poison. Some had then smothered themselves with plastic bags. All of the suicide victims had packed bags with clothes and stuffed their pockets with money. Clearly, they believed that they would need these things where they were going.

The Heaven's Gate cult did indeed believe they were going someplace special: They believed that after shedding their "earthly containers" (their bodies), they would board a spaceship that trailed behind the comet Hale-Bopp. From there, they would be transported to a heavenly kingdom in a far-off galaxy, which they believed would be a "return home." This would allow them to escape the coming end of the world, in which the earth would be "spaded under" by the kingdom of God. The group so looked forward to their journey that they even made videotapes assuring the world that they were happy to be going on to "the next evolutionary level."

The leader of the Heaven's Gate cult, sixty-five-year-old Marshall Applewhite, was a former music teacher who called himself Do and who had quietly led his group since the 1970s. His followers were a collection of mostly middle-aged computer experts and professionals who spent hours on the Internet spreading their beliefs. Applewhite preached that he could teach his followers how to avoid the horrible world-ending Apocalypse that was coming soon. He would give them the information they needed to leave the planet. Group members were strictly forbidden to drink, smoke, or have sex. In preparation for their journey into space, they watched hours of *Star Trek* episodes and the *Star Wars* movies. All of them were cut off from their families.

Apparently, the appearance of Hale-Bopp led Heaven's Gate's members to decide that they had to leave for their outer space journey. But it is also clear that the approaching millennium motivated them to hasten the end. As they said in their final official statement to the world, "We came for the purpose of offering a doorway to the kingdom of God at the end of this civilization, the end of this millennium."

Chapter 7

How Do Other Societies and Religions See the Millennium?

Did the ancient Egyptians believe in the millennium?

The answer to this question depends on whom you ask. Many experts say that the ancient Egyptians, although they believed in an afterlife, did not have any special beliefs about the end of time. However, some modern-day prophets from the nineteenth century on have maintained that the Great Pyramid at Giza, built between 2600 B.C. and 2500 B.C., contains a symbolic timeline that predicts every important date in human history, from Adam and Eve's exile from the Garden of Eden to the end of the world. These prophets claim that an empty tomb inside the pyramid—the King's Chamber—was built for a future messiah destined to appear in the Egyptian priesthood's version of the Second Coming.

We do know for certain that the Egyptians believed in a magical immortal bird, the phoenix. The phoenix would live for five hundred years, after which it would die in a mystical fire and be reborn. The idea of the phoenix is said to be a forerunner to the story of Christ's death and Resurrection. Christian prophets who believe the Great Pyramid foretells the future say there is a passageway within it that predicts Christ's crucifixion in 33 A.D. and a gallery that awaits his return. Some New Age prophets believe that the Great Pyramid was built by aliens; others, like John Hogue, believe that it predicts the end of the world in September 2001.

Who was Zoroaster, and how did he influence millennial thinking?

Zoroaster (also known as Zarathustra) was a prophet and religious leader of the ancient Persian empire, which is now known as Iran. He was born around 628 B.C. Zoroaster is important to the history of millennial thinking because he is believed to have founded the first religion that envisioned a messiah and an End Time. In fact, the religion he founded, Zoroastrianism, sounds very much like Judaism and Christianity. Zoroaster believed that there is only one god, whom he called Ormazd. This is very different from other ancient religions, such as those in Greece and Egypt, which worshiped many different gods.

Zoroaster's teachings were set forth in the Zend-Avesta, a kind of Zoroastrian bible. In it, he taught that Ormazd, who was good, was locked in a great struggle with an evil being called Ahriman. The followers of Ormazd should follow the path of righteousness by leading a good life and doing good works. For this, they would be rewarded after death in a realm of spirit.

Zoroaster's ministry is said to have opened the last of the world's four periods of three thousand years each. Three saviors, considered to be the sons of Zoroaster, would follow him at intervals of one thousand years. The last of these, the Soshyans, would appear at the end of days. During this time, a final battle between good and evil would take place. Good would win over the evil forces of Ahriman, and "the last turn of creation," or the End Time, would occur. All of the living and the dead would be resurrected and judged. The wicked would be destroyed, and the good would live forever—the young to remain always fifteen years old, and the elderly forever forty. Thus, Zoroaster envisioned a kind of Armageddon and Last Judgment very similar to the one found in Revelation, more than six hundred years before John of Patmos wrote it.

What did the ancient Greek philosopher Plato have to say about the millennium?

Plato, the great philosopher, lived between 427 and 347 B.C. His most famous and influential philosophical teachings had to do with the idea of ideal forms. Plato believed that the world was an imperfect and impermanent reflection of an absolute and eternal reality of ideal forms. Man must always strive for this ideal, even if it can never be realized.

Because the idea of the millennium was far in the future, Plato never made any actual pronouncements about it. But he certainly believed in an ideal time that the world would perhaps return to someday. Plato, along with his fellow Greeks, believed that history was divided into four ages: Golden, Silver, Bronze, and Iron. The Golden Age was the perfect age, a kind of paradise. This was when the gods on Mount Olympus had made a golden race of men who lived free of grief and worry and were perpetually young. Plato believed he was living in the late period of the Iron Age—about as far from the ideal Golden Age as you could get! Still, he hoped for a return to that previous, ideal age. And there is some evidence that he believed that someday the world would return to it. He is said to have believed in the Great Year, a cycle of time during which all of the planets would eventually return to their places at the Creation. Perhaps when the planets were at the end of this cycle, history itself would return to the Golden Age. How long did the cycle of the Great Year last? According to Plato, 36,000 years.

Did the ancient Romans celebrate a millennium?

The Romans actually did have a millennium celebration at the one thousandth anniversary of the founding of Rome. Counting from a founding date of 753 B.C. (this date often varied between 759 and 729 B.C., depending on which Roman historian was consulted), the Emperor Philip held a huge celebration in 248 A.D. that lasted many days, during which people danced and drank and held religious ceremonies. It is thought that Philip may have held this millennial party in order to boost the spirits and morale of his people, for it was clear at the time that Rome was in decline. Perhaps like today, some Romans felt that the millennium signaled the doom of the empire. However, Rome did not actually fall until 410 A.D.

But the Romans, like the Greeks, believed in the Great Year—the cycle of the planets that, once completed, would signal both the end of time and a return to its beginnings. According to historians, the Romans were gripped with a fear that the Great Year was about to end whenever Rome was in crisis. Like many twentieth-century premillennialists, the Romans' calculations for an "end of days" would change according to the signs of the times.

Were the ancient Mayans millenarians?

The Mayans are a race of Indians who reside in southern Mexico and Central America. They were the rulers of an advanced civilization located in that area that reached its peak around 1000 A.D. The descendants of this ancient civilization still live in parts of Guatemala and Mexico.

The soothsayers and astrologers of the ancient Mayans observed and recorded the movements of the stars for some four thousand years. The calendar they worked out according to their observations is said to be one of the most accurate in the world. The calendar has its beginning on August 13, 3114 B.C. Months are divided into twenty-day periods, the last five days of which are "bad luck" days. In fact, the ends of months and years in Mayan civilization were regarded with a sense of doom.

Today, many modern prophets are again interested in the Mayan calendar because it predicts the end of a World Age for June 2012. Because it so nearly coincides with the Gregorian calendar's millennium, some people believe that between 2000 and 2012 is the period when global disaster is certain to occur. However, the Mayans believed that the end of a World Age would be not the absolute end but a time of transition followed by greater harmony and peace. So those who predict total destruction for 2012 are misreading the Mayan prophecies.

What is written about the millennium in the Dead Sea Scrolls?

The Dead Sea Scrolls are a collection of parchment scrolls that date from about 100 B.C. to 100 A.D. Most of them were found in caves near the Dead Sea, a salt lake that lies between modern Israel and Jordan. The scrolls contain Hebrew and Aramaic (another ancient language used in the Old Testament) scripture, as well as other religious and nonreligious texts.

Many of the scrolls were written and preserved by a group called the Qumran sect, a Jewish group that lived about a hundred years before the birth of Christ. They appear to have lived a life of denial very similar to that of Christian monks. Not much is known about this group, except that they lived in the desert away from the world and seem to have had strong millenarian beliefs. The scrolls describe a heavenly being called the Son of man, who would descend to save his people. The Qumran sect may have lived in daily expectation of this event, so they might be described as the first millennial cult, even before the time of Christ.

Is there a millennial tradition in the Jewish faith?

In terms of the upcoming millennium, most Jews will doubtless celebrate the milestone as a nonreligious event. On the Jewish religious calendar, the year 2000 will be the year 5757. A new millennium will not arrive until the year 6000, 243 years away.

But if we talk about millenarian tradition in terms of a specific idea about the End Time, Judaism practically invented it. Indeed, even though the origins of millennial thought may have been in the earlier religion of Zoroaster, the Jewish faith was the first to have a highly developed religion based on belief in an End Time.

In the early days of Judaism, which is almost four thousand years old, there was little written about the end of the world. But this began to change when the Jews were subjected to persecution under the Egyptians. Then the idea of a place of deliverance—although not specifically related to the End Time—became common.

The idea of one God, who will deliver his people from suffering into a "land of milk and honey," is first recorded in the Old Testament book of Exodus. Later, the establishment of the kingdom by David in the tenth century B.C. led to a hope in the future Messiah of God appearing from the house of David. This is recorded in II Samuel. The Book of Amos, which was written in the eighth century B.C., records the concept of a "day of the Lord" as a Day of Judgment over all of the wicked of the world. And the Book of Isaiah records a universal judgment combined with the presence of a messiah. This hope for and fear of divine intervention kept the Jewish people united and strong through many times of trial.

But the first detailed picture of what would happen on the Day of Judgment occurs in the Book of Daniel, which was written around 168 B.C., at a time when the Jews were being severely persecuted by the monarch of Syria, Antiochus Epiphanes. Daniel describes all of the empires of the world—including the empire of Antiochus—being destroyed by a force beyond earthly power. Afterward, the Son of man establishes a righteous, just, and eternal kingdom.

This idea of a world-ending battle and the appearance of a divine savior is the forerunner of a similar scenario portrayed in the New Testament book of Revelation. The Book of Daniel was written during roughly the same period that the Qumran sect was discussing a Son of man in the Dead Sea Scrolls. Thus, it is apparent that the idea of a messiah was becoming common throughout the Jewish world shortly before the time of Jesus.

Jews who maintained their faith believed that Jesus was perhaps a wise and good prophet, but not the true Messiah, who was yet to appear. During medieval times, a number of false messiahs gathered followers—much like the many "prophets" in Christianity who have claimed to be the reincarnation of Christ. Today, modern movements in Judaism tend to maintain the traditional faith in an ultimately redeemed world and a messianic future for all of humankind. However, most Jews do not insist on a personal messiah figure; indeed, many Jews do not necessarily believe that a Messianic Age will come.

But like Christians, different Jews have different beliefs about the End Time. Orthodox and Hasidic Jews tend to believe that the Messianic Age will be brought about by an individual leader, while most Conservative and Reform Jews think it will be brought about by the increasing good works of good people.

Do Allah's faithful believe in the millennium?

Like every world religion other than Christianity, the Muslim faith attaches no special religious significance to the year 2000, except that it is the beginning of a new year on the Gregorian calendar. But like those of Judaism and Christianity, Muslim doctrines paint a very clear picture of earth's final days. However, most Muslims do not believe that this day is coming any time soon.

Founded in the early 600s by Muhammad, Islam—as the Muslim faith is also called—has ideas about the end of the world that are similar to those held by Jews and Christians. Muhammad called the final days of time "the hour," and many of his teachings in the Koran—Islam's holy book—revolve around this End Time. Many Muslims today think the last days will be preceded by the rise of a messiah called the Mahdi, who will fight a figure like the Antichrist. Indeed, some Muslims believe Jesus is the Mahdi.

In Islam, the time before the end will be a period of moral decline. God himself will abandon the godless world. Ka'bah, the great place of pilgrimage in the Muslim world, will disappear; copies of the Koran will become empty paper, and its words will be forgotten. The earth itself will finally disintegrate; the law of gravity will weaken, and the earth will begin to shatter. As this happens, all humankind will be resurrected for God's Final Judgment. Good people, Muslim and non-Muslim alike, will be sent to paradise. Others will go to hell for a period of purification, and then they will enter paradise, too. Only the truly evil, along with Satan, will remain in hell.

What are some Hindu beliefs about the millennium?

Because the concept of time goes in cycles in Hinduism, there is no belief in an ultimate, destructive end to the world and humankind. Rather, life is an endless series of cycles—birth, death, and rebirth. Humans are endlessly reincarnated from one generation to the next. The only escape from this cycle is for individuals who achieve a final, enlightened state called *moksa*.

But even in Hinduism, there is a sense that the world will get progressively worse before the cycles begin again. The first cycle is the Age of Light, or the Krita Yuga—a time of perfection and holiness. This is the longest cycle, lasting 1,728,000 years. The second cycle is the Treta (Three Fire) Yuga, lasting 1,296,000 years; the third cycle is the Dvapara (Doubt and Uncertainty) Yuga, lasting 864,000 years; and the fourth is the Kali (Dark) Yuga, lasting 432,000 years. As the name suggests, this last cycle is the darkest period of time, when misery prevails and humankind goes into decline. According to Hindu teachings, we are currently living through this Kali Yuga. However, different teachers have different calculations about exactly where we are in the Kali Yuga.

Some New Age prophets insist that the Kali Yuga will end in the year 2000, at roughly the same time that the Age of Aquarius begins. They believe that the end of Kali Yuga will usher in a Golden Age of light. But people have been predicting different dates for the end of Kali Yuga for many years. Some people believe it ended in 1898; others say it won't end until 2442. Apparently, when believers talk about cycles of time that last many thousands of years, the correct date cannot be consistent.

Do Buddhists believe in the millennium?

No. As in Hinduism and other Asian religions, the concept of time is cyclical in Buddhism. Escape from the cycle is possible only for the enlightened individual who reaches Nirvana, a state of complete bliss. But there is no millennium in the sense of the coming of the Messiah or a Final Judgment for all humankind.

However, some believe that the turning of the Buddhist cycle of time will coincide with the year 2000. Buddhists envision time as a great wheel, the Wheel of Dharma (or law), which turns every 2,500 years. The wheel is a symbol of Buddha himself, whose name was Gautama Siddhartha and who founded the faith around 500 B.C. He represents a perfect being that has no beginning and no end.

In his book *Prophecies for the New Millennium*, James Manning explains that "each turn of the wheel brings about a new vision for mankind that slowly comes to fruition, fades away, and is followed by another vision of the future." The next turn of the wheel is due at the dawn of the third millennium and "will bring about a new beginning with many changes and new awakenings, possibly even the advent of The Lord Maitreya—the Buddha who is yet to come—and the creation of a new harmony on earth."

Do Native Americans have a millennial tradition?

The diverse tribes of Native American Indians have varying beliefs about both the end of time and the upcoming millennium. As we saw in chapter 6, the Ghost Dance Movement of the late nineteenth century combined Christian belief about the millennium with Native American rituals. It was embraced by a number of tribes all over the West at a time when their lands were being taken away by white settlers and the U.S. Army. The movement ended in tragedy when it turned out that the Ghost Dance did not deliver Native Americans from the bullets of the white man.

But the upcoming millennium also has called forth some specific predictions by contemporary Native American prophets. For example, a Lakota spiritual leader named Arvol Looking Horse, along with a council of Native American elders, has organized prayer days in preparation for the year 2000. The Day of Prayer is organized around the summer solstice in June and is in response to ancient prophecies that the earth is in grave danger unless people return to spiritual ways before the millennium. Prayer days are open to anyone who wishes to devote time to learning to live in harmony with the earth and with each other. The Lakota and the Plains Indians believe that unless people learn to live in balance with nature, global disasters await us in the coming years.

Perhaps the most famous Native American prophet of the millennium is Sun Bear, a Chippewa medicine chief who died in 1992. He was the author of *Black Dawn, Bright Day*, a book of prophecy that combines his own visions with traditional Native American prophecies. In perhaps his most famous prediction for the millennium, he compares the earth to a shaggy dog with fleas. At some point, the dog must shake itself violently to get rid of the fleas. This, Sun Bear said, is what will happen to the earth. The earth will erupt in a violent spasm to protest what humans are doing to it. The world's cities will become prey to race riots and natural disasters: "The planet will survive, even though perhaps millions of people will perish."

The only way to escape the coming disaster, according to Sun Bear, is to change one's way of life and move to the countryside. Sun hats, umbrellas, and warm clothing will be necessary to prepare for the extreme weather changes that will occur. But for the people who abandon the cities, the changes to come "will be very positive and good for all of creation. It will be the beginning of a new age for those willing to change themselves."

Chapter 8

Were There Signs in the Year 1000?

What is the big controversy over the first millennium?

What really happened on the eve of the year 1000? It is a question that historians have been arguing about ever since the eighteenth century. To hear some experts tell it, in 999 A.D. fear and anticipation of the coming millennium was so great that all of Europe was in a panic. Signs of doom were everywhere: Torrential rains, floods, and epidemics swept over the land. People everywhere sold all of their possessions and rushed to the holy city of Jerusalem to greet the Second Coming. In fact, the road to Jerusalem was so clogged with pilgrims that it looked as if an entire army was marching through. On New Year's Eve 999, the churches were filled with trembling souls awaiting the end. When it failed to come, the world went wild with joy. Whole countries converted to the Catholic faith in gratitude that the earth had been saved from destruction.

The idea that great, momentous events surrounded the year 1000 has long been a part of the millennial folklore. But some time late in the nineteenth century, historians began to question whether anything at all special had happened in 999 A.D. They concluded that it definitely had not. They believed that the stories of great panic and upheaval had been completely made up by earlier historians. Ever since then, experts on the Middle Ages seem to have gone in the opposite direction with their picture of the millennium. Not only did nothing special happen, not only did people *not* believe that the world was coming to an end, most people didn't even know what year it was! Some historians of the Middle Ages don't even mention the year 1000 at all, as if to prove that the millennium had absolutely no meaning or significance to anyone.

Lately, however, experts are once again taking a closer look at what really happened a thousand years ago. With interest and excitement about the coming millennium reaching a peak, historians are renewing their investigations into the way our ancestors reacted to the last one. Strangely enough, they say the idea that nothing happened in the year 1000 is nonsense. Maybe there wasn't widespread panic, but some people were indeed warning that the world would end, and other people reacted to this news accordingly.

So what is the truth about the year 1000? Maybe we will never know. Records and written testimony from that period are few. When they exist, they are incomplete and often contradict each other. This is why different experts have so often disagreed about what happened.

But it's certain that controversy and interest in the year 1000 will only increase as the time of our own millennium draws closer.

Did people living in the year 1000 know what year it was?

The answer depends on which expert you ask. Some historians say that peasants in the tenth and eleventh centuries had no idea of time in terms of an actual date on a calendar. They didn't even use calendars, and since they could neither read nor write, they would not have known *how* to use them anyway. Their only way of telling time was by natural means: The average peasant knew it was time to get up when the sun rose and time to go to bed when the sun set. They knew to plow and plant their fields in the spring and to harvest them in the fall. As for the lords and landowners in society, these same historians say that each used a different system for telling time, usually according to how long the current king had been in power, and that there was no common agreement about what year it was.

However, other historians point out that the *anno Domini* ("in the year of the Lord") calendar—which counts time from January 1, 1 A.D., the supposed day of Christ's circumcision—had been in use since the sixth century, when the monk Dennis the Short invented it. In every church and monastery throughout practically all of Europe, priests and monks used this calendar to calculate the date of Easter. They were very much aware of what year it was. Further, historian Richard Landes points out, peasants would have been ignorant of what year it was only if they chose not to know. He thinks it is very likely that many Christians at that time would have known the year because they were concerned about the arrival of the millennium, which they were afraid might bring the end of the world.

Were there signs of a Second Coming?

There certainly were events that people believed were signs of the Second Coming. Damian Thompson, in his book *The End of Time: Fear and Faith in the Shadow of the Millennium*, says that in 1033 a monk named Richard Glaber wrote *Histories*, a five-volume history of the millennium. The book sets down, according to Glaber, "the story of the events and prodigies [wonders] which happened around and after the millennial year of the Incarnation of the Saviour." And, according to Glaber, there were many "events" that were read as signs in the year 1000.

Seven years before the millennium, as Glaber tells it, nearly all of the cities of Italy and Gaul (today's France) were devastated by "violent conflagrations"; Rome itself was destroyed by fire. Many prominent nobles and priests died. Glaber tells the tale of a community of monks who experienced an earthquake as they were celebrating Easter in the year 1000. Shortly after that, a comet appeared in the sky for three months. And historian Hillel Schwartz notes in his book *Century's End*, "Near the close of the millennial year, a French peasant claimed to have been possessed by a swarm of bees, who inspired him to chase away his wife, trample crucifixes," and refuse to pay the church taxes!

In other words, just as in our own day every natural disaster or strange event is used by some prophet as proof that the end is near, so the people of the eleventh century saw any disaster as a sign, too. The usual comets, floods, earthquakes, fires, and even a swarm of bees were all signs that the Day of Judgment was at hand.

Did the Bible predict the Second Coming for the year 1000?

No. As was noted before, there is no place in the Bible that predicts the time of the Second Coming. But the idea that a unit of one thousand years had passed since the birth of Christ would have struck a chord with Christians of the time, who were very familiar with the Bible's book of Revelation and its reference to the thousand years of Christ's reign on earth.

What were the "terrors of the year 1000"?

This is the phrase historians use to describe the widespread panic and fear of the Second Coming that were supposed to have overcome Europe at the time. As we've seen, some experts believe that the terrors are a myth—that they never happened. But how did those who did believe them describe them?

One eighteenth-century historian claimed that "a general consternation seized mankind; many relinquished their possessions, and abandoning their friends and families, hurried. . . . to the Holy Land, where they imagined that Christ would quickly appear to judge the world." Another historian in the nineteenth century, Charles Mackay, wrote:

> In the year 999, the number of pilgrims proceeding eastward, to await the coming of the Lord in that city [Jerusalem], was so great that they were compared to a desolating army. . . . Buildings of every sort were suffered to fall into ruins. It was thought useless to repair them, when the end of the world was so near. . . . Knights, citizens, and serfs traveled eastward in company, taking with them their wives and children, singing psalms as they went, and looking with fearful eyes upon the sky,

which they expected each minute to open, to let the Son of God descend in his glory.

In his book *Doomsday, 1999*, Charles Berlitz wrote that in the year 999, people forgave each other's debts and prisoners were released from jail in anticipation of the end. While some pilgrims whipped themselves on the road to Jerusalem, others saw visions of flaming swords and arrows streaming through the sky and committed suicide in great numbers, "as people sought to punish themselves in advance of Doomsday or simply could not stand the pressure of waiting for Judgment Day." Still others write that in December 999, shopkeepers closed their stores, peasants left their fields, and children were sent home from school to prepare for the coming Apocalypse. On New Year's Eve 999, the masses huddled in churches and under great crucifixes in the fields to await their doom.

Did such scenes actually take place? We may never know for sure. But such stories will doubtless continue to be told about the year 1000. What will people be saying about the "Terror of the Year 2000" a thousand years from now?

What did Christians believe about the end of the world in the year 1000?

We do not know for sure whether a general panic over the end of the world actually took place in the year 1000; probably it didn't. But even so, we can be sure that Christians during the time of the Middle Ages thought about the end of the world a great deal more than most of us do today. The book of Revelation and its detailed descriptions of the End Time were familiar to the average person from countless church sermons, paintings, statues, and folk tales that vividly depicted the events of the return of the Antichrist, the terrible Battle of Armageddon, and the Last Judgment.

In the Middle Ages, religion was interwoven with every daily event; the world of spirits, angels, and devils was an ever-present reality to people of all walks of life. As people sought to make sense of the usually grim circumstances of everyday life, the idea of the end of the world was both a source of terror and a source of promise. The Antichrist would come and inflict destruction on the world. Terrible torture and damnation awaited, but then the sweet promise of the kingdom of God would be fulfilled. And signs that the events of the final days were about to begin were everywhere. Every natural disaster or catastrophic event was read as a sure symbol that the end was near.

Perhaps this is why so many historians do not believe that the "Terrors of the Year 1000" happened. In fact, they argue, the terror that the world would end and that the events described in Revelation would unfold was always real to people living at that time. In this respect, the turn of the millennium was no different than any other time in the early Middle Ages.

What was the Peace of God Movement?

The Peace of God Movement took place in the late tenth and early eleventh centuries. It is one of the events that historians point to in order to demonstrate that the time surrounding the millennium was different from other times. It started in France in the 990s, at a time when a great number of relics—pieces of clothing or the actual remains of saints and martyrs—from the early years of the church were discovered. Great crowds of people gathered in fields to worship at displays of these relics. At many of these open-air gatherings, it was reported that miraculous healings took place. Bishops and priests took the opportunity to organize the crowds into a movement calling for peace among the landlords and noblemen, who were constantly at war with each other over land rights. Soon the cries of "Peace! Peace! Peace!" were heard in the fields, as thousands of peasants, knights, and nobles gathered to pray for a new age of peace. Crowd members often fell into ecstasies and had visions. People repented of their sins, and lords swore oaths of peace in front of all present.

This peace movement lasted into the 1030s. Some historians, including Richard Landes, believe that it was a response to fears and hopes revolving around the period between 1000 and 1033, the one thousandth anniversary of Christ's Crucifixion. Were members of the Peace of God Movement praying to bring on the Last Judgment? Did their vision of an age of peace mean the lasting peace of the millennial kingdom? Many experts think it did. And so something like a mass response to the millennium actually did take place—in the Peace of God Movement.

Did people celebrate the millennium in the year 1000?

There is no record of people "celebrating" the first millennium in the sense that we use the word today. In other words, it is doubtful that people held big parties or marked the passing of the year 999 with any unusual festivities or events. If we are to believe historians, people were either cowering in churches in fear of the Second Coming or quietly going about their business with no knowledge that something special was happening.

But according to Richard Glaber, the monk who wrote *Histories* in 1033 to document the events surrounding the millennium, there was a kind of celebration *after* the millennium:

> Just before the third year after the millennium, throughout the whole world, but especially in Italy and Gaul [France], men began to reconstruct churches, although for the most part the existing ones were properly built and not in the least unworthy. But it seemed as if each Christian community were aiming to surpass all others in the splendour of construction. It was as if the whole world were shaking itself, shrugging off the burden of the past, and cladding itself everywhere in a white mantle of churches.

Were people celebrating the fact that they had survived the millennium by renewing their faith in God? Was the sudden building of churches a sign of joy that the dreaded Day of Judgment had not arrived? This seems to be what Glaber is suggesting. If so, then in a sense it can be said that people celebrated the millennium.

Did panic over the millennium cause the Crusades?

Since the first Crusade didn't take place until the year 1096, it seems pretty unlikely that the Crusades were undertaken in response to the millennium in 1000. But it is clear that some people who joined the Crusades did so in expectation that they were bringing on the biblical millennium.

The Crusades were military expeditions undertaken by Christians all over Europe to recover the Holy Land from the Muslims, who had captured and held Jerusalem since the fifth century. The Crusades lasted more than two centuries, as knights and beggars, lords and peasants took up the banner of the cross and marched east, often destroying everything and everyone in their paths. Many of the poor left their homes to go on a Crusade, knowing they would never return. But for them, the Crusades held the promise of escape from a miserable existence and of salvation. Pope Urban II, who called for the first Crusade, had promised that anyone who died during the battle would gain forgiveness for all of his sins—an instant ticket to heaven.

To this promise, another hope was attached: Once the Crusaders rid Jerusalem of Muslims, the New Jerusalem of Revelation would miraculously appear. Many people, especially the poor, believed that participation in the Crusades was a way to bring on the events foretold in Revelation. For them, the Muslims represented the forces of the Antichrist, and they were riding to the Battle of Armageddon. Once victory was won, God's kingdom on earth would appear. In light of the hopeless poverty at the time, the thought of a glorious new heaven on earth was well worth risking one's life for. In this respect, then, the Crusades really were a millennial event.

What were some of the great historical events in the year 1000?

In truth, no really great historical events took place in the year 1000, especially in Europe. At that point in time, Europe was a backward, rural society made up of dozens of "petty kingdoms just emerging from the chaotic Dark Ages that followed the Visigoths' sack of Rome in 410," as an essay in *Life* magazine described it. Peasants were virtual slaves to the lords who owned the land. They mostly lived in mud and thatch huts and survived on a sparse diet without benefit of flavorings such as sugar, salt, and spice. They slept on the floor with their animals and huddled around wood fires for warmth. They lived in constant fear of barbarians who would sweep over the land, stealing and killing. Another threat was disease of every kind, particularly tuberculosis and plague. Most peasants of the tenth century did not live beyond age 30.

The nobility of the day had an easier time of it, but their lives were usually taken up with constant battles over land. They lived in cold, drafty castles made of timber. Many of them could neither read nor write. The only sign of enlightenment was in the monasteries, where monks composed and owned the few books that existed.

The Islamic empire—which stretched from southern Spain and northern Africa to southeast Asia—was far more civilized. Scholars studied medicine, mathematics, and physics; libraries were common. Another great civilization was flourishing in China, where artists and scientists thrived and important inventions such as gunpowder and the compass were about to change the world.

But these distant civilizations were little known in Europe until trade to the East began to open up in the twelfth and thirteenth centuries. Perhaps the greatest event of the time was Leif Eriksson sailing from Greenland to North America—the longest sailing expedition up to that time. Unfortunately, news of this adventure never reached beyond northern Europe. Thus, the millennium passed uneventfully, at least in terms of historical events.

What are some important historical events since the year 1000?

In 1997, *Life* magazine published a special double issue in which the editors ranked the one hundred most important events of the past millennium. Here are the top ten events, in order of importance:

1. Gutenberg prints the Bible. *Life* magazine calls the printing of 200 typeset Bibles in 1455 the most important event of the millennium. Johannes Gutenberg was the first person to mass-produce books. He made the first movable-type system in the West and chose to produce copies of the Bible as his first printing venture. Before then, books had to be produced by wood-block printing or by hand, both painstaking processes that took a great deal of time. This meant that books were rare and available only to a tiny group of nobles, priests, and scholars. Most people did not have any access to the printed word. Although Gutenberg's process was still fairly slow (it took one day to set the print for a single page), it led to rapid improvements in his invention. By 1500, a half-million printed books were in circulation. Ordinary people had access to all kinds of information and ideas. Political and religious revolutions, such as Martin Luther's Protestant movement, spread much more quickly than they ever could have before Gutenberg's invention. The printing press truly changed the entire course of history.

2. Columbus created a global civilization. According to *Life* magazine, the second most important event of the past millennium is Christopher Columbus's voyage to the New World from Spain in 1492. Columbus first landed on an island in the Caribbean, which he named San Salvador, on October 12 of that year. Although Columbus was arrested in 1500 for mismanaging the island and sent back to Spain in chains, his discovery of a world across the sea opened the way for more exploration of the Americas.

3. Luther knocks down the door. In 1517, Martin Luther nailed his Ninety-Five Theses to the door of All Saints Church in Wittenberg, Germany. The theses were an extended criticism of the Catholic Church and the pope's authority, which at that time was not only spiritual but political. The pope was the supreme authority of all Europe. But after Luther, both the people and kings and princes began to rebel against the church. Protestantism was born, and the authority of individual nations became more important than the church. To this day, the separation of church and state means that most countries are ruled by governments that do not have religious affiliations. This is because Luther broke the political authority of the church in 1517.

4. The machine age gears up. In 1769, James Watt patented the steam engine. The invention of this machine forever changed the way the world works and paved the way for the Industrial Revolution. The steam engine is what made railroads, steamships, and factories possible. Before then, most manufacturing had been done by hand, and most people lived on farms or in small towns. By 1870, 70 percent of the people in rural England had moved to cities to work in factories. City populations exploded, along with slums, overcrowding, and widespread disease. But mass-produced goods and the cost efficiency of machines also brought about higher standards of living, greater convenience, and hundreds of inventions that changed the way people lived.

5. Galileo sees the moons of Jupiter, and the earth moves. Galileo Galilei, the great astronomer, was born in Italy in 1564. He did not invent the idea that the earth revolved around the sun, but he did improve the telescope enough that he could prove this was true. In 1610, he saw the moons of Jupiter through his telescope, demonstrating that both the earth and Jupiter revolved around the sun. At the time, it was believed that the earth did not move and was the center of the universe. In fact, Galileo was placed under house arrest by the Catholic Church for demonstrating that this was not true. He was forced to take back his ideas about the earth. But he is said to have muttered under his breath "And yet it [the earth] does move" when he was told to claim the opposite.

6. Scientists develop the germ theory of disease. Until the mid-nineteenth century, nobody knew what caused diseases to thrive in the human body. At one time, it was even thought that evil spirits were the reason people became sick. But in the nineteenth century, it was discovered that infectious agents multiply inside the body, and that is what causes illness. In 1865, French scientist Louis Pasteur discovered that these infectious germs are present in the air. Finally, in 1876, German scientist Robert Koch demonstrated that specific germs cause specific diseases. From then on, scientists could begin making vaccines against these microorganisms. They began to realize that sanitary conditions and proper hygiene are crucial to disease prevention. These discoveries, as *Life* reports, "did more to increase the life span of humans than any other scientific advance of the past one thousand years."

7. China develops gunpowder weapons. China discovered the formula for gunpowder in the ninth century. When gunpowder reached Europe in the 1300s, it changed the power structure of the land forever. Kings, the only ones who could afford large supplies of guns, began forming armies. Backed by these armies supplied with guns, the kings took control of the individual fiefdoms that had been ruled by nobles. Consequently, the domination of the nobility declined. Instead of being divided among many little territories run by nobles, power became centralized in nation states, each ruled by a king.

8. America makes a declaration to the world. The Declaration of Independence, written by Thomas Jefferson and adopted by the Continental Congress of the United States on July 4, 1776, is the document that laid the foundation of democracy. The idea that "all men are created equal" was revolutionary at the time. No other country had ever been founded on such an idea. All democratic movements and countries have been based on the principles of the Declaration of Independence ever since it was written.

9. Hitler comes to power. The atrocities committed by Adolf Hitler and the Nazis have no equal in the course of human history. Seventeen million soldiers and 60 million civilians died during World War II. Most horribly, the Nazis systematically murdered 6 million Jews in death camps. The scale of Hitler's evil forever changed what people imagined was possible. But as *Life* points out, Hitler's wickedness had unexpected consequences. When Germany lost the war, the United States and the Soviet Union became the world's superpowers. The United Nations was founded. And the State of Israel came into being in 1948. These events changed the course of twentieth-century history.

10. The compass goes to sea. Although the compass was invented in China four centuries before the birth of Christ, it did not reach Europe until around 1190. At that time, it began to be used in the West as a guide to navigation on ships. Before then, sailors had only the stars to guide their course. But the compass made long-term voyages possible; sailors no longer had to worry about cloudy skies. Without the compass, the great sea voyages that led to the discovery of the New World could not have taken place. In other words, no compass, no America.

Life magazine also compiled a list of what it considers the ten people who contributed the most to the millennium (in order of importance):

1. Thomas Edison
2. Christopher Columbus
3. Martin Luther
4. Galileo
5. Leonardo da Vinci
6. Isaac Newton
7. Ferdinand Magellan

8. Louis Pasteur
9. Charles Darwin
10. Thomas Jefferson

Other people would doubtless choose other places and people as the most important of the past millennium. But there is no question that the past one thousand years have brought enormous changes in the way we live our lives. World population has jumped from 300 million to 5.9 billion, and life expectancy for the average person has climbed from age thirty years to sixty-two. Europe, which a thousand years ago was living in darkness and illiteracy, grew to become the most influential civilization on the earth. European explorers discovered the Americas, and today, the United States is the leader among nations. The voyage across the sea that once took many months of hardship now takes place hundreds of times a day in a matter of hours. And people on one side of the globe can communicate with those on the other side in a matter of minutes.

If a person born a thousand years ago could wake up in today's world, imagine the wonders that would greet him. If we could wake up to the world a thousand years from now, what wonders would greet us?

Chapter 9

What If Computers Crash?

What is the Y2K problem?

The Y2K problem is shorthand for the year 2000 problem, also known as the millennium bug. What's the problem? Well, unless they are fixed, all computer programs everywhere will crash at 12:01 A.M. on January 1, 2000. Of all of the doomsday scenarios that prophets and soothsayers have imagined, the Y2K problem is the one that has the most chance of actually happening. And if it *does* happen, the results could be catastrophic.

Why exactly might computers crash? Simply put, because they won't know what year it is. When computers first became commonly used in business during the late 1960s and early 1970s, they were very expensive. One of the most expensive costs involved storing data. Even storing one or two extra characters of data could cost many hundreds of dollars. So when it came to storing the date, computer programmers used only enough characters to store the last two digits of any given year. In other words, the date May 20, 1998, is stored as 052098 instead of 05/20/1998. This saves four characters of data space, including the slash marks and the "19." The computer automatically reads the year as 1998. This is fine... until the year 2000 arrives. Because there is no storage allotted for the crucial first two digits of the year, any computer that is not reprogrammed will automatically read any year as 19—. For example, January 1, 2000, will be read as 010100, or January 1, 1900.

Thirty years ago, no one expected that the computer programs they were writing would still be in use in the year 2000. Unfortunately, they were wrong. Most major computer applications still use the same code that was invented in the early years of computer programming. Unless corrected, computers will reset to 1900 or some random year, or they may simply mistake "00" for "not available." All of the activities computers control today will malfunction or stop.

How difficult is it to fix the Y2K problem?

If the only thing that needs to be corrected on computers is the date, why can't programmers simply put two extra digits into the dates in the computer programs? Unfortunately, fixing the Y2K problem involves more than just sticking the two extra digits into the dates. It involves, first of all, finding every single date in a given computer program. As computer expert Peter de Jager explains, there is no easy way to find all of the dates registered in a computer program. Correcting computer systems for the Y2K problem means, in most cases, looking for dates through every bit of programming that has been done over the past thirty years. The average company that uses computers will have programs containing more than 100,000,000 lines of computer code. Every single line of code must be searched for the date. De Jager explains that if a person spent only one second looking at each line of that code, it would take more than thirteen years to look through all of it! And after all of the dates in all of the programs are fixed, each program and piece of software will have to be tested. Obviously, correcting the problem is a time-consuming and costly task.

What will happen if the Y2K problem is not fixed?

As de Jager warns, the Y2K problem will affect all information stored in computers that is based on time. Your driver's license, credit cards, insurance cards, Social Security card, invoices, subscriptions, warranties, drug expirations, and the like are all based on two-digit expiration dates. When the year 2000 arrives, all of the data banks that contain information for these cards will think that the expiration year occurred in the twentieth century, not in the twenty-first. An expiration date of 01, for example, will be read as 1901, not 2001.

Worse yet, interest calculations also could be thrown into chaos. Imagine finding out that one hundred years of interest has been added to your loan because the bank's computer reads the year 2000 as the year 1900. But the problems won't end there. Virtually every aspect of our lives could be affected if the Y2K problem is not fixed. Power outages could occur; traffic lights could fail to work; water and sewage treatment facilities could shut down; air traffic control could come to a halt; satellites could fail. The possibilities are nearly endless, given the thousands of systems that are controlled by computers.

ABC News recently prepared a study of the YK2 problem. The report envisioned eight different possible scenarios of what could happen if computers crash in the year 2000:

* The computerized elevator controller in your office building could decide that no maintenance has been done on the elevator in one hundred years and could lower all of the cars to the ground floor, as it would do in case of a fire. People who decide to take the stairs might find that the building's security system won't recognize their cardkeys, locking people out of the stairwells.
* Your bank's computer might miscalculate and give you one hundred years' accrued interest on your account. Or it could register that you are one hundred years overdue on your loan payment.
* Your credit card, which has an expiration date of 2000 or higher, could be declined or rejected if the merchant's terminal miscalculates the expiration date as 1900.
* Your airline reservations could be canceled automatically because the airline computer could read them as having expired one hundred years ago. But the airline is in chaos anyway because the computer system has already recorded that no planes need service and that the crews aren't properly trained.
* Many jails have computer systems that classify prisoners according to criminal history, physical and mental condition, and the level of risk for housing placement. On January 1, 2000, these jails could automatically reject new prisoners and mistakenly miscompute the release dates of prisoners already behind bars.

* Telecommunications industries that do not fix their Y2K problems could totally fail. The phones might not work. Even if they do, the embedded software instructions burned into the computer chips on many fax machines could misread dates and times, making fax transmissions late or undeliverable.
* Prescriptions phoned in by your doctor at the end of 1999 may have already expired by the first days of 2000 if your pharmacy's Y2K problem is not fixed. In addition, computerized medical systems could omit crucial dates on your medical records or lose your records completely.
* Calls to fire departments, which usually track the times of calls by computer, could be recorded by the fire departments' computers as already answered. This could cause an endless number of glitches and backups in emergency services of all kinds.

Indeed, it is almost impossible to imagine all of the possible problems the Y2K issue could cause if it is not fixed.

Do computers need to be reprogrammed before the year 2000?

Many computer experts believe that they do. In fact, in order to be safe, computers should be reprogrammed by December 31, 1998. This is because the changes made to computer systems will have to be tested for a full year to make sure that all of the applications used during the course of a year will work. If problems do arise, companies will need time to figure out how to fix them—and how long it will take to fix them—as far in advance of the year 2000 as possible. Companies that have already begun to fix their Y2K problems have found that the project requires much more time and manpower than originally estimated. Waiting until the last minute is not an option.

Can computers be reprogrammed in time for the millennium?

It's possible, but already it seems very unlikely that all computer systems will be reprogrammed in time for the year 2000. When de Jager wrote his informational essay "You've Got to be Kidding!" on the Y2K problem in early 1997, only 35 percent of all American businesses had even begun to fix their computer systems. In Europe, less than 10 percent of all computer systems were being fixed. And in Asia, the percentage was even smaller. At those rates, we can expect that many companies will fall short of the year 2000 deadline, much less the safe deadline of December 1998.

Financial analysts at the Gartner Group predict that at least half of all companies will have computer problems on January 1, 2000. Even if a company's internal computers are fixed, it could have trouble doing business because of problems with telecommunications networks. Regional phone companies contain more than 70,000 programs that need replacing, and experts say that they cannot be fixed on time. Even many government agencies, such as the Departments of Treasury and Defense, are far behind schedule in fixing their Y2K problems.

To complicate matters, many businesses believe that only their mainframe computers need to be fixed. (The mainframe is the original or "legacy" computer that was programmed back in the early days of the computer revolution and never replaced.) But this is not the case. Servers—the powerful computers that control vast networks—and PCs and laptops within the individual companies will probably need to be reprogrammed as well. A company may have 100,000 desktop computers and servers, each loaded with software that may or may not be equipped with the programming to handle a four-digit year. Ignoring this vast world of computers within a company will definitely mean that even companies that think they've solved their Y2K problems could be in trouble.

Some companies are waiting for someone to come along at the last minute with a simple cost and time-effective solution to the problem. Unfortunately, most experts agree that such a solution will not arrive. Those companies that wait will find themselves on the brink of disaster come December 31, 1999. In fact, any company that has not already begun to work seriously on its Y2K problem is probably already too late to fix it on time.

How long will it take?

We have already estimated that it would take more than thirteen years for one person to look at all of the computer code in a single business's programming. And that's just looking at the code to find all of the dates that need to be fixed. Fixing or reprogramming the code will take even longer. At this point, entire companies have been created to deal with other companies' Y2K problems. But even companies that employ fifty people who do nothing else but fix computers probably will still need several years to complete the task. For example, the Bank of America, the fifth largest bank in the United States, hired one thousand people to work full-time on fixing the bank's 200 million lines of code two years ago. They are less than half-done with their task. Will they finish on time? It's possible that they won't.

Of course, the answer to how long fixing the Y2K problem will take depends on each company's size and the original programming it used. And now there are some tools available that can automatically change some of the codes in old computer programs. But even so, the task of reprogramming computers is, in most cases, a matter of years, not months.

Will the stock market crash if computers are not reprogrammed?

It's possible. First of all, stock markets may simply shut down because the automatic trading systems they depend on may fail if their computers are not reprogrammed. Second, it is difficult to imagine that a widespread computer failure won't affect stock values as a whole. Bankruptcies and bank failures are already being predicted as a result of the Y2K problem. If enough companies go under, this could indeed cause a plunge in the stock market.

Some investors already are preparing for the Y2K problem by diverting their stocks away from companies that might suffer collapse from computer meltdown. Instead, they are investing in companies that have been created to fix Y2K problems. This is a booming new business, as hundreds of companies are forming to work exclusively on fixing other companies' computer troubles.

However, investment in these companies could cause another problem down the road. This is what stock experts are calling the year 2001 problem. What happens when those companies set up to solve the Y2K problem succeed at their task—and find themselves out of business by 2001? Investors in these companies could suffer huge losses when the Y2K problem goes away. The stock market could suffer an even greater downturn in 2001.

How much will it cost to correct all of the computers in the world?

According to de Jager, the rough guideline being used in the industry is that it costs $1 to correct one line of computer code. At this rate, some experts estimate that the worldwide cost of fixing the Y2K problem will be between $300 billion and $600 billion. Others say that those numbers are too low—the cost will be double that. Consider the following sums that individual companies and government organizations are spending on fixing their Y2K problems:

The United Kingdom:	$5.04 billion
Bankers Trust New York Corporation:	$230 million
The State Government of California:	$200 million
J. P. Morgan and Company:	$155 million
The Toronto Stock Exchange:	$33 million
Florida Power and Light Company:	$25 million
Dayton Hudson Department Stores:	$14 million

This is one very expensive problem!

Will the Y2K problem cause a recession?

It could. Experts say that Y2K-related failures will cost the U.S. economy $120 billion in lost output between now and the year 2001. Why? Because the time, money, and staff that could have been dedicated to making products or providing other services will have instead to be put to work solving the Y2K problem.

The Millennium Investment Corporation, a U.S. investment company, is predicting a global recession starting in late 1999. They claim that failure to fix computer systems could cause widespread disruption in the business community and act as a catalyst for world recession. The corporation is advising businesses of all kinds to prepare for an economic downturn destined to arrive by the year 2000.

Senator Robert Bennett of Utah claims that a recession will be caused not by the Y2K problem itself but by the cost of lawsuits that will result from it. Imagine all of the lawsuits that could be filed, for example, because of the personal injuries that computer failures might cause. Imagine shareholders suing companies for stocks that plummeted because they failed to fix their Y2K problems. Imagine those companies suing the people who were supposed to fix their computer problems and didn't. Imagine individuals suing companies for the business losses caused by the Y2K problem. The scenarios for legal problems are virtually endless.

Some experts say that for every dollar spent fixing year 2000 bugs, there will be $10 in legal costs. So if the worldwide cost of fixing Y2K is estimated at $3 billion to $6 billion, legal costs could total $3 trillion to $6 trillion! To get an idea of how much money that is, the U.S. economy's total output is $7 trillion. The effect on the economy could be staggering.

What can you do to prepare?

Unfortunately, since it is unlikely that all businesses everywhere will have fixed their computer problems before the year 2000, even people who do not work in computer-operated businesses should be prepared for the worst. The worst may not happen, but the more ready we are for possible breakdowns and glitches, the better off we will be.

What could happen when January 1, 2000, rolls around? Well, utilities such as phone, gas, and electricity could be shut off if local utility companies do not correct their computers. Social Security and pension checks may not arrive on time. As of December 1997, the Social Security Administration reported that it faced computer problems that could threaten its ability to provide assistance to millions of people. Although the administration began preparing for Y2K problems almost ten years ago, it still may not be ready for the next millennium. Finally, people who have mortgages or loans—especially with small or mid-size banks—could find that the calculations on these loans are incorrect come January 1, 2000. Smaller banks may not have the money or resources to deal with the Y2K problem in time for the millennial deadline. Given the number of date-related transactions that financial institutions deal with, these small banks and credit unions may even collapse. What can you do to prepare for these and other scenarios?

* First, contact your employer, bank, insurer, and anyone else who holds computer records of your financial affairs. Ask them exactly how they are preparing for the Y2K problem and when they expect their computer systems to be fixed. If you are not completely satisfied with their answers, switch to the services of another company that is dealing with the Y2K problem.
* Next, keep complete and thorough paper records of all of your financial affairs through 1999. Make sure that these records are correct, and put them in a safe place before the end of December 1999.
* If you have or receive a credit card with an expiration date of 00 or later, keep all transaction slips and check them carefully against the statement the card company sends you.
* Keep all of your utility and phone bills, so you have proof of meter readings and phone calls made before and around the year 2000.

* If you are buying or renewing an insurance policy, check with your broker or insurer to see if your policy has any year 2000 exclusions. Are you covered for year 2000 accidents and glitches?
* Test home appliances that have date-sensitive timers, such as videos and fax machines. Set the clocks on these devices to roll over from 1999 to 2000. If they do not work, take them back to the retailer. This is especially important if your appliances will be more than six years old in the year 2000. It was just six years ago that some appliance makers began to incorporate date-sensitive mechanisms in their products.
* Find out if your salary, your Social Security benefits, and your pension can be paid in cash or by check in January 2000.
* Make sure you have enough cash, food, fuel, and heating for a few weeks at the beginning of the year 2000, in case a major computer meltdown takes place in your community.

Will your personal computer need to be reprogrammed?

Probably, especially if it is more than a few years old. And unless you regularly update your software, it's likely that you will have to upgrade at least some of it. The good news is that fixing a home computer is not nearly as difficult as reprogramming company computer systems. As long as your home PC is not attached to a larger computer network or mainframe, the task is fairly easy. And the consequences of failing to reprogram your PC will probably be fairly minor: data spreadsheets, personal financial records, and calendars will be inaccurate, but your system will not experience a meltdown.

As computer expert Caron Golden notes, Apple Mac or Mac OS-compatible computers are already programmed for the year 2000. Older models, such as Apple II, will probably need to be loaded with Pro DOS 8 Version 2.0 or later to ensure that your applications will handle dates after the year 2000. It's a good idea to check with an Apple dealer or to visit Apple's Web site at product.info.apple.com to find out about the individual model you own.

If you own a PC that is less than a few years old, it is probably programmed for the year 2000. But it is a good idea to check your basic input output system—or BIOS—and your built-in hardware clock to make sure. As Golden reports, a Pennsylvania company called National Software Testing Laboratories has developed software to test if the BIOS in your computer is Y2K-ready or if it will need an upgrade. The software is free and easy to use and can be downloaded from the company's Web site at www.nstl.com.

If you're using an operating system such as Windows 95 or Windows 98, you probably have nothing to worry about when the year 2000 rolls around. But if you use Windows 3.1 or 3.11, your file manager will incorrectly display the date after January 1, 2000. It's time to upgrade to Windows 95 or 98.

For software, it's best to check the Web site of the maker of your various brands of software—whether it's Lotus, Intuit, Microsoft, Claris, Starfish, or something else. You'll find information about whether an upgrade is needed and how to change the datefields on your current software. Problems may arise, however, when you share data with others whose PCs are not year-2000-ready. In other words, even the most thorough, conscientious PC users may find that the Y2K problem will catch up with them one way or another!

Chapter 10

Is America Ready?

Why does the millennium have special meaning in America?

We have seen throughout this book how the coming millennium has become associated with the idea of a Golden Age. Many people believe that the year 2000 may bring the thousand-year reign of Christ that is spoken of in the last book of the Bible, Revelation (also known as the Apocalypse and the Apocalypse of John). These ideas probably are more popular in America than anywhere else on earth, in part because America is the most religious nation in the world. But the ideas in Revelation also present a common theme that has been sounded throughout America's history.

From the moment of its discovery, America has been associated with visions of a new age and a promised land that have very strong millennial feelings behind them. It is only natural, then, that as the new millennium approaches, many Americans—whether or not they are religious—seem to feel strongly that the dawning of the year 2000 will mean something special.

For example, when Christopher Columbus first caught sight of the New World in 1492, he declared, "God made me the messenger of the new heaven and the new earth of which he spoke in the Apocalypse of John." In other words, from its birth, America was seen as the New Jerusalem. This idea was taken up by the Puritans, who arrived here from England in the seventeenth century and who founded the colony that is now Massachusetts. They spoke often of America, where they had come to escape religious persecution, as the New Jerusalem. It was a shining "city on the hill," a phrase that was borrowed centuries later by politicians such as President Ronald Reagan to describe the promise of America. Puritan writings about the New World also depict scenes from Isaiah, where the lion and lamb lay down together. Truly, America was seen as a special place in which all of the hopes of the early settlers would someday be fulfilled.

When Julia Ward Howe wrote the "Battle Hymn of the Republic" in the nineteenth century, she used phrases from Revelation such as the "fateful lightning of his terrible, swift sword" to describe the freeing of the slaves during the Civil War. Progressive Christians used ideas from Revelation when they described the need for child labor laws at the beginning of this century. And in the 1960s, Martin Luther King said he had "seen the promised land" in his vision of an America of racial and religious tolerance.

The history of America is the history of people who hope for and work toward the peace and harmony of a perfected world like the New Jerusalem of the Bible. As a country that is always looking toward a better future, and as a country that was founded with the purpose of making a better world, it is no wonder that America looks forward to the celebration of the next millennium with special excitement.

Are fears and hopes about the year 2000 more intense in America?

They seem to be. Certainly, there is a large number of groups and religious sects in America that believe something special will happen in the year 2000. In fact, a recent opinion poll revealed that more than 100 million Americans believe in at least some parts of the prophecies described in Revelation. As the millennium approaches, many of these people's beliefs about the End Time are becoming more intense.

But the sense of celebration and excitement also seems to be more intense in America. Most American cities are planning special year 2000 events and celebrations. The biggest one will be the Times Square party on New Year's Eve 1999. More than a million people will be gathered there to welcome in the new millennium, and another 250 million will watch the event on TV. Americans everywhere will doubtless take the opportunity to celebrate the biggest New Year's Eve in history by holding the biggest parties.

Other countries, on the other hand, have not done much preparation for the millennium. For example, Russian President Boris Yeltsin only recently decided to make an official announcement about planning for the millennium. But there is no sign that he or anyone else in Russia is certain about how or even *if* the country will prepare official celebrations. France has planned some official events, but a recent poll there found that 50 percent of the French people feel they will be less well off in the next millennium than they are now; in other words, they are not in a celebrating mood. Japan and other Asian countries are planning no official celebrations, probably because even though the Gregorian calendar is used in the East for business, their holidays are based on their religious calendars. In addition, the Asian economy is not doing very well right now; Japan and southeast Asian countries are in no mood to celebrate. In Australia, the government has put off the millennial celebration until 2001—the year of the one hundredth anniversary of the Australian constitution. In the year 2000, the country will be caught up in the Summer Olympics in Sydney.

There are probably only two other places in the world that are preparing celebrations on a scale equal to or greater than the ones expected in America: at the Vatican in Rome and in London, England. The Vatican, of course, is preparing to celebrate the two thousandth birthday of Christ. It expects more than 30 million people to visit the Holy City during the course of the year. In London, the British government is building a huge Millennium Dome that will cost $1.3 billion. The dome will be a giant celebration site during the millennial year and is expected to draw 12 million visitors. But in England, the dome has been widely criticized because of its cost and because nobody knows exactly what should go on inside it to commemorate the new millennium. Controversy over the dome has somewhat dampened British enthusiasm for the year 2000 celebration.

In America, however, ideas about how to celebrate the millennium are being welcomed in every community and will encompass many ideas about the new era—both religious and nonreligious. And because America is currently experiencing a very prosperous and healthy economic climate, most people will probably be in the right mood to hold giant parties come New Year's Eve 1999.

How are Americans preparing for the millennium?

In America, there probably are as many preparations for the year 2000 as there are Americans. Officially, the U.S. government has initiated an ambitious White House Millennium Program that will include many special events, goals, and projects throughout the year 2000. Some of them include the following:

- President Bill Clinton has set a goal of connecting every classroom and library in the United States to the Internet by the year 2000.
- The National Endowment for the Humanities will sponsor a nationally televised series of "Millennium Minutes" that highlight one thousand years of important people, events, and achievements. The National Endowment for the Arts also will earmark funding for twenty-nine special millennial projects, including a program to send teams of photographers across the country to capture their visions of America at the brink of the new millennium.
- The President's Committee on Arts and the Humanities will launch the Worthy Ancestors program, which will be saving significant cultural materials from American folk, popular, and classical traditions.
- The National Archives will launch a three-year project to ensure that the original Constitution, the Bill of Rights, and the Declaration of Independence are preserved for the next millennium.

* The Smithsonian Institute will launch the Save Our Star Spangled Banner by 2001 project, which will be devoted to preserving the original flag that flew over Fort McHenry and that inspired Francis Scott Key to write the poem that became our national anthem.
* President Clinton is sparking an initiative to continue support for our explorations of space by the National Aeronautics and Space Administration, which will launch new missions to Mars in 1998, 2001, and 2003.
* The National Science Foundation is sponsoring its Year 2000 program, a national campaign on the importance of science, engineering, and mathematics.
* AmeriCorps, the national service program, has set a goal of doubling the number of full-time AmeriCorps volunteers by the year 2000.
* The White House is inviting all Americans to share their ideas about celebrating the millennium by visiting its official Web site at www.whitehouse.gov.
* The best local projects commemorating the millennium will be awarded special titles as Millennium Communities over the next three years.
* The government-sponsored radio program Voice of America will begin a series of special broadcasts around the world about how the United States is celebrating the millennium.
* The president recently underscored America's sense that it has a special place in the next millennium when he delivered these words at the White House Millennium Event:

  For centuries, people have wondered what this millennium would bring. Would it signal an Apocalypse or herald a new world, mark a time of decline or a time of renewal? Whatever the prophecies and forecasts. . .

whatever the hopes and fears, the millennium is no longer a distant possibility. It has arrived. We are present at the future, a moment we must now define for ourselves and for our children. As the year 2000 draws near, we must ask ourselves: What will it take to meet that challenge, to define that future, to prepare ourselves for a new century and a new millennium? Thomas Paine said a long time ago, "We have it in our power to begin the world over again." We have always believed that in this country, and we must now take it upon ourselves to take stock as we approach this new millennium to commit ourselves to beginning the world over again for our children, our children's children, for people who will live in a new century.

What is the Millennium Watch Institute?

The Millennium Watch Institute is a foundation in Philadelphia that keeps track of and provides information on more than 1,100 American groups and cults, specifically those groups that prophesy global change or catastrophe in the near future. The institute was founded in 1992 by Ted Daniels, an author and folklorist who has written a great deal about the millennium and the growth of prophetic cults and groups. Daniels collects the literature written by and about these groups and publishes a newsletter about them called the *Millennial Prophecy Report*. The University of Pennsylvania in Philadelphia will store Daniels's collection of literature on cults in its library, so that people who want to find out more about these groups will be able to do research there.

The Millennium Watch Institute and the *Millennial Prophecy Report* have been credited with finding out information about the Branch Davidians and the Heaven's Gate cult long before anyone else. For anyone who wants to know about or keep track of groups that are predicting the end of the world for the year 2000, the Millennium Watch Institute is an invaluable resource. It has a Web site at www.channell.com.

What is the U.S. Time Capsule Monument?

The U.S. Time Capsule Monument will be one of the more unusual millennial events to commemorate the next thousand years. A huge monument is being constructed in the Boston Mountain Range in Winslow, Arkansas. The structure will store millennial time capsule cylinders that are made to last for the span of the next millennium. To ensure preservation, thick walls of glass, plastic, concrete, and steel will separate each cylinder. The halls connecting the chambers will be filled with sand. The only way to remove the contents of the "millennium chambers" will be to take apart the entire monument. Winslow, Arkansas, was chosen as the site because it is earthquake-free, high in altitude, mild in temperature, and isolated from any military targets.

Anyone who wishes to leave something behind for the year 3000 can purchase a time-capsule cylinder. Those who buy cylinders can fill them with their life stories, videotapes, journals, voice recordings, and any other items and documents about themselves—presumably to be opened a thousand years from now by distant relatives or curious historians. Purchasers also will have their names engraved on the outside of the monument and will receive instructions on how to create a lasting time-capsule cylinder. In addition, they will have their own personal Web sites with pictures, audio, and links about themselves and the contents of their time capsules. Anyone interested in becoming a part of the U.S. Time Capsule Monument can contact its Web site at www.ustimecapsule.com.

How has the millennium been depicted in science fiction?

Over the years, there have been many science fiction books that portray the world sometime in the next millennium. As the year 2000 approaches, there will doubtless be many more such depictions. But there certainly is no common or consensus view of what the world will look like come the millennium. Some visions paint an ideal society blessed with peace and full of wondrous technological marvels; many more depict a world devastated by war or overrun by alien invaders.

One of the most famous visions of life in the next millennium is British author Aldous Huxley's *Brave New World*, which was written in 1932. Huxley's novel takes place in the twenty-sixth century or, as the novel puts it, in 632 A.F.—(after Ford), 600 years after Henry Ford became the pioneer of mass production. In this world of the future, children are conceived in factories and raised in "state conditioning centers." There they are conditioned to believe that "everybody's happy now." There are no parents and no marriage; people mate only for sex. Children are separated into different categories of intelligence before they are born and can never strive to change the way they are. Inhabitants of this brave new world have ready access to a drug called Soma, which makes them feel good all of the time but which also makes it impossible for them to get close to others or to question their lives. Strong emotions such as love are bred out of the test-tube babies. Still, some of the inhabitants who have not been totally conditioned to accept their society try to escape.

Sixty-five years after it was written, Huxley's novel has proved to be remarkably accurate about some things that have happened. For example, sheep and other animals have been cloned, just as humans in *Brave New*

World are mass-produced. Test-tube babies have already arrived. Huxley's novel describes women wearing birth-control belts around their waists, at a time long before birth-control pills were invented. Soma, which the characters in *Brave New World* take to make them happy, has been compared with today's antidepressant drugs such as Prozac. Huxley even foretold the connection between alcohol and fetal birth defects. But Huxley's greatest fear for the future was that totalitarian governments would completely control the lives of their citizens and that technology might destroy the world. At the time he wrote, the rise of Adolf Hitler was only just beginning, and the start of World War II was several years away. Huxley's vision almost came true.

Another, earlier, book about the millennium paints a totally different picture of life in the twenty-first century. The American Edward Bellamy wrote his novel *Looking Backward, 2000–1887* in 1888. It is about a man who falls asleep in the nineteenth century and wakes up on September 10, 2000. Set in Boston, the novel depicts a millennial age in which there is no war, no violence, no pollution, no inequality, and no poverty. People are well off and work at jobs of their choice. After age forty-five, people are free to retire and enjoy a life of leisure. Incredibly, Bellamy's future world describes a time when everyone carries around credit cards instead of cash and shops in malls where people can buy every product imaginable under one roof. Clock radios with headphones are common, and electric heat and light are everywhere. This vision of the future was so popular that *Looking Backward* became the bestselling book of its day.

More recent books about the coming millennium have turned to doomsday scenarios. For example, *The Last Day* by Glenn Kleier, which was published in 1997, describes the mysterious destruction of a secret Israeli defense laboratory on the eve of the millennium. An investigative TV correspondent discovers that the lone survivor of the laboratory explosion is a young woman named Jeza. Millenarian groups all over the world soon hail Jeza as the Messiah, and she becomes the leader of a global religious movement. But Jeza may really be a robot with artificial intelligence. She is destroyed near the Wailing Wall as Armageddon-like violence spreads through the Middle East on Good Friday of the year 2000. But Jeza is destined to be resurrected on Easter morning—unless someone can stop her.

Another recent book that depicts a grim scenario for the next millennium is Douglas Coupland's *Girlfriend in a Coma*. Its heroine is seventeen-year-old Karen McNeil, who falls into a coma in 1979 and wakes up at the end of the twentieth century. Karen is horrified by the changes the world has undergone; nobody seems to care about the future or have dreams of a better life. All anyone cares about is money. Karen herself begins to have terrible visions of the future. She confesses her visions on television, and soon afterward, the world comes to an end. But the end does not come in a fiery Armageddon. Instead, everyone falls asleep and dies, until no one is left alive except for Karen and her friends. They must make their way through this desolate world until an old friend comes back from the dead to help.

Perhaps the best vision of the new millennium will be found not in a book but right here in reality, when the Science Fiction Hall of Fame opens early in the year 2000. Shaped like a giant flying saucer, it will be built on a 45-acre tract of land at Long Beach Seaport in California. Forrest J. Ackerman, owner of the largest collection of science fiction artifacts in America, will display some of his collection there. The Science Fiction Hall of Fame reportedly will be loaded with special effects.

What are some of the movies and television shows about the millennium?

As we approach the millennium, Hollywood seems to be turning out more and more movies about major disasters that will occur in the near future. The past few years have seen movies such as *Independence Day*, in which aliens invade the earth and blow up the White House (along with nearly everything else in the world), and *The Fifth Element*, in which a futuristic cab driver saves the world from a galactic evil force. *Armageddon* features a giant asteroid that is hurtling toward earth at 22,000 miles an hour. A team of men is sent into space to stop it—and to prevent Armageddon. In *End of Days*, Satan comes to New York City on the eve of the millennium in search of a bride. An ex-policeman, played by Arnold Schwartzenegger, engages the Antichrist in a life-and-death struggle on New Year's Eve 1999.

What are some other movies that have depicted life in the next millennium? Ridley Scott's 1982 film *Blade Runner* takes place in the Los Angeles of 2019—a grim, polluted city where Detective Deckard, played by Harrison Ford, is sent on a mission to destroy "replicants," human clones who are threatening to rebel against the totalitarian system that runs the world. And 1973's *Soylent Green* portrays an overcrowded New York City in 2022, where 40 million starving people struggle to survive. Pollution has taken its toll, and the homeless, jobless inhabitants must survive on a food substitute called soylent green—which is made, sickeningly enough, of other people.

But the most famous movie set in the near future is probably Stanley Kubrick's *2001: A Space Odyssey*. The 1968 film about man's exploration of the frontiers of space amazingly predicted a world where space shuttles are routine, voice-activated IDs are used for security clearance, and a supercomputer named HAL 9000 beats his human companions at chess. A full year before the first trip to the moon, 2001 depicted a moon walk that looked almost exactly like the real thing. The movie, which was based on a short story by science fiction writer Arthur C. Clarke, was probably most frightening in its portrayal of HAL, a computer so diabolical that it outsmarts and eventually kills one of the astronauts on the space mission.

Television, after portraying future worlds in cartoons such as *The Jetsons* and adventure series such as *Lost in Space* and *Star Trek*, has recently turned to depicting a more violent, sinister vision of the near future. *Millennium*, a show created by Chris Carter, of *The X Files* fame, represents a dark world of evil conspiracies and satanic plots. The main character, Frank Black, is an ex-FBI agent who has the ability to see into the minds of serial killers and other evildoers. He tries to escape the world of crime, but a secret organization called the Millennium Group recruits him to help stop the terrible, violent events that threaten to destroy the world in the upcoming millennium. The show presents one of the most disturbing visions of what's ahead as we approach the year 2000.

How is the millennium being celebrated on the internet?

If you do a search of the word *millennium* on the World Wide Web, you are likely to turn up about 250,000 "hits"—

or contacts—devoted to celebrating or exploring the year 2000. There is probably no other place where the upcoming millennium has caused more excitement and concern. Here you will find all kinds of cults, UFO-seekers, religious groups, political activists, and ecology groups that believe the world will end within the next few years. And you will find groups like the Millennium Watch Institute, devoted to keeping track of these end-of-the-world people. There also are organizations like Talk 2000, Millennium 2000, and the Institute for Millennial Studies, which are devoted to studying and providing all kinds of information about the millennium. Any of these sites will in turn lead you to at least a dozen or more additional sites about the millennium.

If you'd like to count down the seconds to the next millennium, the Millennium Clock, a Java-powered timepiece on the World Wide Web, will be there to help you do it. The clock will run down as random images from the world's past two-thousand-year history flash up in the background. Anyone in the world with a web browser will be able to download the clock free of charge.

And if you're stuck with no place to celebrate as the new millennium rings in, you can go to the New Year's Eve Parties' 2000 site, which lists all of the planned celebrations for the year 2000 all over the world. Information on public gatherings is listed there, as well as invitations from private citizens who are having parties and simply want anyone and everyone to drop in. But it's probable that the biggest party on New Year's Eve 1999 will take place on the Internet, where thousands of people throughout the world will be glued to their computer screens as the clock strikes midnight.

What are some businesses and products named after the millennium?

Name a business or product, and a millennium brand probably exists. Here is just a random sampling:

Millennium Broadway Hotel
Millennium Chemicals
Millennium Communications
Millennium Computer Corporation
Millennium Cruises
Millennium Energy
Millennium Film Workshop
Millennium Hilton
Millennium Media
Millennium M&Ms
Millennium Mortgages
Millennium Pharmaceuticals
Millennium Publishing
Millennium Screensavers
Millennium Software
Millennium 2100 Gas Fireplaces
Millennium Virtual Airlines
Millennium Water Filters

How long will we celebrate the millennium?

Way back at the beginning of this book, we discussed why some people say that the millennium will not arrive until the year 2001. Technically speaking, there is no year 0, so the countdown to the thousand-year turning point actually starts in the year 1 A.D. and ends in the year 2001.

This provides a good excuse for people to celebrate the millennium for a whole extra year. In fact, the country of Australia has decided to hold off all of its official millennial celebrations until 2001. But even after the last streamer and party hat have been swept away on January 1, 2002, some people probably will find other excuses to keep celebrating the new millennium. And why not? After all, if we don't take advantage of the opportunity now, we'll have to wait another thousand years.

Bibliography

Banks, Adelle M. "No Date Set for Second Coming." *The Plain Dealer*, September 2, 1995.

Beers, Carole. "Native Americans Ride, Walk to Devil's Tower." *The Seattle Times*, June 19, 1996.

Bowman, David. "Fears of Computer to Human Virus Transfer." *The Scotsman*, April 1, 1998.

Britannica Online. Encyclopaedia Britannica, Inc.: 1994-1997.

Cabbage, Michael. "Earth: A Giant Celestial Target." *Sun-Sentinel*, April 12, 1998.

Carlin, John. "Welcome to World War III." *The Independent*, February 22, 1998.

Chua-Eoan, Howard G. "Life in 999: A Grim Struggle." *Time*, October 15, 1992.

Cohn, Norman. *The Pursuit of the Millennium.* New York: Oxford University Press, 1971.

Davis, Bob and David Wessel. *Prosperity.* New York: Times Books, 1998.

Davis, Brett. "NASA is breathing new life into search for extraterrestrials." *Houston Chronicle*, April 6, 1998.

de Jager, Peter. "You've Got to be Kidding!" Year 2000 Information Center, January 10, 1997.

The Economist. April 18, 1998, U.S. Edition.

Eliade, Mircea, ed. *The Encyclopedia of Religion*. New York: Macmillan, 1987.

"Experts Agree: We're Finished." *New York Times*, January 19, 1997.

Fauber, John. "Scientists debate Earth's top threat." *Milwaukee Journal Sentinel*, January 26, 1998.

Goering, Laurie. "Guyanese Jungle Reclaiming Jonestown." *Chicago Tribune*, May 10, 1997.

Golden, Caron. "Will 2000 be the year that breaks the clock?" *San Diego Union-Tribune*, October 14, 1997.

Gould, Stephen Jay. *Questioning the Millennium*. New York: Harmony Books, 1997.

Graham, Billy. *Approaching Hoofbeats: The Four Horsemen of the Apocalypse*. Waco, Texas: Word Books, 1983.

Hadfield, Peter. "Japanese cult in subway killing is back." *USA TODAY*, April 2, 1998.

Hogue, John. *The Millennium Book of Prophecy*. San Francisco: HarperCollins, 1994.

Jacobs, David M. *The Threat*. New York: Simon & Schuster, 1997.

Johnson, Dan. "Virus hunters pursue our invisible enemies; infectious diseases." *The Futurist*, January 11, 1998.

Johnson, K. Paul. *Madame Blavatsky and the Myth of the Great White Lodge*. Albany: State University of New York Press, 1995.

Jones, Helen. "Tomorrow's World." *Creative Review*, March 2, 1998.

Landes, Richard. "Apocalyptic Expectations around the Year 1000." Center for Millennial Studies, 1996.

Lattin, Don. "Apocalypse Meets Millennium in Texas Sect." *San Francisco Chronicle*, March 7, 1998.

Lawson, Tracey. " 'Scientific Philosopher' Hopes to Create Lots of Identical People." *The Scotsman*, April 2, 1998.

Maney, Kevin. "Lawyers circling over 2000 time bomb." *USA TODAY*, December 1, 1997.

Mann, A.T. *Millennium Prophecies*. Shaftsbury: Element Books Limited, 1992.

Manning, James. *Prophecies for the New Millennium.* London: Thames and Hudson Ltd., 1997.
Marquand, Robert. "2001: A Millennial Odyssey." *Christian Science Monitor*, January 7, 1998.
"Mega Events Planned for 2000." Millennium Alliance/Millennium Institute: 1996-1998.
"Millennium Bugged." Special Report, ABCNEWS.com, 1998.
"Millennium Mania." *Family Circle*, January 1998.
"The Millennium: 100 events that changed the world." *Life* Magazine Special Double Issue, Fall 1997.
Mysteries of the Bible. Pleasantville: The Reader's Digest Association, Inc., 1988.
O'Sullivan, Arieh. "Virtual Terror: Threat of a new world disorder." *Jerusalem Post*, March 27, 1998.
Popcorn, Faith. *Clicking*. New York: HarperCollins, 1996.
Ramsay, William M. *The Westminster Guide to the Books of the Bible.* Louisville: Westminster John Knox Press, 1994.
Robbins, Thomas and Susan J. Palmer, eds. *Millennium, Messiahs, and Mayhem.* New York and London: Routledge, 1997.
Rosenblatt, Robert A. "Latinos May Hold Key to Future of Social Security." *Los Angeles Times*, March 25, 1998.
Savage, Marshall T. *Millennial Project.* New York: Little Brown, 1994.
Schwartz, Hillel. *Century's End.* New York: Doubleday, 1990. "Generational Change, Historical Age, Calendar Page." Millennium Institute, 1996.

Thompson, Damian. *The End of Time*. Hanover and London: University Press of New England, 1996.
Ulin, David L. "The UFO Believers' Secret Desert Mecca." *San Francisco Chronicle*, March 26, 1998.
Von Sternberg, Bob. "Millennial Musings." *Minneapolis Star Tribune*, October 25, 1997.
Woodward, Kenneth L. and Jennet Conant. "Witness for the Millennium." *Newsweek*, October 15, 1984.

About the Author

Linda Moore was born in Cleveland, Ohio. She received master's degrees from The Johns Hopkins University (non-fiction writing) and from Case Western Reserve University (English). At Ithaca College she directed and taught in the school's writing center. At Johns Hopkins she taught film and consumer culture and non-fiction writing. Moore is a free-lance writer, editor, and film critic and a contributing editor for *In These Times* and for *Baltimore Magazine*. She currently lives in Baltimore with her husband.

